UNIQUE EATS AND EATERIES

OF

DENVER

Library of Congress Control Number: 2018962448
ISBN: 9781681061979

Book Design: Barbara Northcott
Photos credit of the author unless otherwise indicated.

Printed in the United States of America
19 20 21 22 23   5 4 3 2 1

UNIQUE EATS AND EATERIES

OF

DENVER

CHAD CHISHOLM

Hope you enjoy!
~ Chad

DEDICATION

To the marvelous Mile High City and the unique and
fantastic fare found there.

CONTENTS

ACKNOWLEDGMENTS

A heartfelt thank-you to all those who helped make this book an actuality. A love for food and culture, nightly outings, and an expanding knowledge of the industry makes every experience unique, especially with family and friends while exploring the ever-expanding city offerings. Much appreciation to the chefs and producers who pour themselves into their craft simply to share with eager eaters who keep coming back for more. A special thank-you to JT, my ever-patient spouse for listening to my ideas and copy, helping me through the process of writing this book, and encouraging me along the way. Thank you, too, to Shannon and Lois, helping hands that helped orchestrate a very large undertaking.

INTRODUCTION

Growing up, we didn't go out much to eat locally. Eating out was reserved for very special occasions, as it is for many families—a milestone birthday dinner, a landmark anniversary, or a huge accomplishment were regularly accompanied with dining reservations. Otherwise, we'd cook and eat in for most meals. Now, as a food writer and photographer, my senses are filled with creative culinary opportunities. It is still special for me, albeit far more often, to enjoy a meal out. Denver has always held a very distinct place in my heart, as I grew up just outside the city in the small mountain community of Evergreen. As the Centennial State continues to grow, so does the culinary scene; we had 247 restaurants open in 2017 and over 230 in 2018 according to our visitors bureau. This allows for a wide array of various experiences, a competitive field for not only culinary excellence but also service and ambiance that vies for customers' appreciation.

The ninety eats and eateries found within are a representation of many fantastic places found in Denver, with more appearing all the time. I made a point to find a wide variety of opportunities about which to write, and I know some Denver favorites are not included here. Yet I hope you glean some information or stories you may not have heard, learn more about a particular spot, or simply enjoy the collection presented in these pages.

Something that strikes me about the culinary scene in Denver is the dedication to giving back to the community. Far from run-of-the-mill charitable contributions or annual small donations, more often than not restaurants and food purveyors here go above and beyond the call of duty, donating time and funds to local charities and communities on a regular basis. From matching donations to creating scholarships at local schools, from partnering with paid internship programs to participating in Dining Out for Life with

Project Angel Heart, the culinary community also runs deep in the sense of family and teamwork within the organizations. Many restaurants offer 401 (k) plans to employees, benefits that exceed industry standards, and travel to foreign destinations to ensure the food is authentic and provides inspiration.

The history of Denver plays not only into the rich fabric of the culture here but as a siren song for those looking to create their own new home. Whether a multigenerational restaurant that continues its traditions or an entrepreneurial spirit coming to Colorado from either coast or from across the ocean, Denver is home to a plethora of unique stories, sublime recipes, and ambiance that is as carefully crafted as the menu.

It is something special to witness when cheesemongers light up and enjoy their work as they explain to customers the art of their craft or a butcher shows patrons how they make the cuts; the sense of wonder and pride in their work is evident in the gastronomic culture throughout the city and surrounding areas.

Far from the Wild West days of campfire cookouts and local meats only (although be sure to try these!), our restaurants now boast fresh fish from across the globe, exotic fruits from far-off places, spicy Indian curries, and creamy European cheeses, not to mention a robust craft brewery scene to wash it all down. The Mile High City continues to inspire and aspire to new heights. I hope you enjoy the many offerings of the city and the stories of how they came into existence in *Unique Eats and Eateries of Denver*. Bon appetit!

—CC

UNIQUE EATS AND EATERIES
OF
DENVER

COURIER.
MARKET | BAR | KITCHEN

Newspaper inspired

Papers fly off the newspaper press, inky tomes of daily news, the air thick with anticipation. In a heated race with the competing newspaper, the inaugural issues were printed within twenty minutes of one another, and the race continued for almost 150 years. Built on the very spot of one of Denver's founding newspapers, courier. market | bar | kitchen pays homage to the historical locale.

The canopy of an abstracted printing press towers over diners entering the space, small nooks with filing cabinets converted into dining room tables, desk task lamps of the editor's office now a chic lighting element, and nods to an era when newspapers were the only source of keeping up with events of the day.

Cocktail menu items, such as the "Front Page" and "Limited Edition," are passed over shining black stone countertops, antique typewriters the backdrop for market items, and newspapers of today lined out for guests to browse. The breakneck speed of the newsroom has become a leisurely dining spot as courier. market | bar| kitchen offers rewritten takes on culinary classics that don't need editing.

1750 Welton St.
303-603-4171
courierrestaurant.com
Neighborhood: Downtown

Follow @courierdenver on Instagram for images fresh off the press

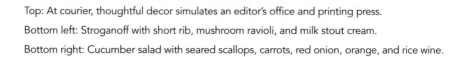

Top: At courier, thoughtful decor simulates an editor's office and printing press.

Bottom left: Stroganoff with short rib, mushroom ravioli, and milk stout cream.

Bottom right: Cucumber salad with seared scallops, carrots, red onion, orange, and rice wine.

TAG RESTAURANT

Continental social food

Denver's TAG Restaurant is one of Larimer Square's distinctive dining destinations.

Housed in the Joe Replin Building, named for the owner of a nearby office supply store for more than fifty years, the space had been a false-fronted building that was a pool hall and a magnet for drunken commotion.

TAG takes its name from chef/owner Troy Atherton Guard. TAG's unique cuisine can be described as a culinary journey—food that is unconstrained by national boundaries—drawing from Chef Guard's Hawaiian upbringing and his travels to Asia and Latin America. The restaurant's cuisine blends local ingredients and international inspiration. After finishing college and going on to train at each of the La Costa Resort's five restaurants in San Diego, he returned to Hawaii and soon became sous chef to the famed Roy Yamaguchi. Blending California, French, and Japanese traditions with Yamaguchi, Guard refined his unique Pacific Rim cooking style as chef de cuisine at acclaimed Doc Cheng's in Singapore. Troy Guard also worked with Latin American chef Richard Sandoval at Zengo Restaurant in the Riverfront Park neighborhood.

A surprising find in landlocked Denver, the OG Taco Sushi two-bite ahi tuna taco with mango salsa served on hand-smashed

TAG restaurant group continues to grow, with eight concepts currently in several locations throughout Denver.

4

Above: The OG Taco Sushi with charred Hawaiian ahi, sushi rice, guacamole, and li-hing mango salsa.

Right: Larimer Square is home to historic buildings with intricate facades.

guacamole has become a staple of the restaurant and a Denver go-to dish, as has the miso black cod with its buttery delicious, melt-in-your-mouth texture.

1441 Larimer St.
303-996-9985
www.tag-restaurant.com
Neighborhood: LoDo

ANNETTE

Field of dreams

Poppies speckle the interior, the bright red painting on the wall mirrored in the steel cutouts in the space. Chef Caroline Glover's grandfather painted the piece, and the integration into the restaurant feels as seamless as the ease in which she brings ingredients to life.

Named after her great-aunt Annette, the restaurant opened in 2017. Oak wood is stacked along the wall to feed the wood fire, which 75 percent of the food touches in some way. A simple, small menu is ingredient and seasonally focused, allowing for the space and food to talk for itself.

Partnering with DeLaney Community Farm, the organic ingredients and sense of community grow deeper. A project whose mission is to support refugees through sustainable agriculture, the 158-acre historic property in which the project farms is right off the Highline Canal. The farm provides space, support, and education to families to grow healthy, organically produced food for themselves and their communities. Dignified experiences and economic resiliency are promoted through the program, and educational experiences in all aspects of farming are taught.

2501 Dallas St., #108
720-710-9975
www.annettescratchtotable.com
Neighborhood: Stapleton

"We seek to do as little to the food as possible and really let the ingredients shine." –Caroline Glover

6

Top left: Fresh, seasonal ingredients pop with color at Annette.

Top right: Toast with plums, torn basil, and goat cheese.

Bottom: Beauty meets function in firewood storage and comfortable dining spaces.

BEATRICE + WOODSLEY

A meal among the aspens

Sunset in Colorado is usually a breathtaking experience—the Rocky Mountains a backdrop to "God's paintbrush" in fiery reds and oranges, deep blues, and royal purples. Capturing the experience, owner Kevin Delk melds nature and dining into one on South Broadway, transporting guests through space and time.

One of the first to offer small plates in Denver, the now bustling culinary scene of South Broadway didn't always used to be so elevated. Adult video stores, dusty antique shops, and used bookstores were a far cry from the walkable neighborhoods of today, with high-end dining, luxury apartments, and sought-after real estate. Opening in 2008 as a fine-dining establishment, Beatrice + Woodsley pioneered the Denver scene, sometimes to their own chagrin, introducing the small-plate concept of several flavor profiles to guests ordering more than one entrée.

Also informing the culinary approach was women's suffrage and the immigration patterns from the 1870s to 1920s. Far from re-creating authentic dishes to the recipe of the time, Delk aims to bring attention to the food science happening during the period. Instead of spending hours and sometimes days preparing food, new products were being introduced to the home cook and culinary scene alike that allowed for quicker preparation times and modified recipes. This in turn freed up time for home cooks to pursue other interests and causes.

Previously an upholsterer's loft, the exposed brick walls and rustic interior pair with the elegant and whimsical fabric treatments, slim lines of cured aspen trees (harvested by Delk and his wife in groves of trees sustainably), and reclaimed wood elements throughout the

Left: Reclaimed wood helps visitors feel as if they are dining among the aspens.
Right: Escargot and crunchy bread.

space. Chainsaws support beams behind the bar, and unique pulls for the bathroom sinks make for memorable design elements.

Beatrice & Woodsley is inspired by the story of two lovebirds: Beatrice, the life-loving daughter of a French winemaking family, who relocated to California in the 1800s to create a small vineyard, and Woodsley, the handsome and crafty son of lumberjacks turned coopers, who provided barrels for the fledgling wine producers. Upon first sight, Beatrice and Woodsley fell in love and quickly married. Stirred by his new bride, Woodsley built a remote cabin amid the woods of the Colorado mountains. Built with skilled and loving hands, Woodsley constructed a strong abode complete with the day's amenities and a large wine cellar between the roots of the aspens. Life was lived with appreciation and happily ever after among forest birdsongs and snow-capped peaks.

38 S. Broadway
303-777-3505
www.beatriceandwoodsley.com
Neighborhood: Baker

PARISI PIZZERIA, TRATTORIA E VINO

Pizza perfection

Simone and Christine Parisi originally opened a small, authentic Italian market in 1998. With edible nostalgia offered daily, the house-made mozzarellas, hard-to-find preserved goods, and genuine Italian meats were too popular for the small space; expansion was inevitable. Eventually landing in their Tennyson location, the deli, takeout, and fast casual concept upstairs is mirrored by an authentic Tuscan fine-dining experience downstairs, Firenze.

The crackling wood-fired oven greets guests upon entering the warm and inviting Parisi Pizzeria, Trattoria e Vino. Italian spoken by many of the staff transports diners to another country. Paninis galore grace the menu, and handmade pastas, such as the gnocchi sorrentina or tagliatelle ragu, leave guests mopping up rich red sauce with grilled bread. Sweet gelatos beckon from a gleaming case, with novelties from Italy on display and for sale to take home to attempt to re-create the Italian flavors found within Parisi.

4401 Tennyson St.
303-561-0234
www.parisidenver.com
Neighborhood: Berkeley

Tennyson Street Cultural District offers an Arts Walk the first Friday of every month.

Top left: Italian classic caprese salad and customer favorite *coccoli* (pizza dough fritters with Stracchino cheese and prosciutto).

Top right: Parisi's wood-fired pizza oven.

Bottom left: A nod to the original Parisi: a small market with imported Italian goods such as pastas, cookies, espresso, and so much more.

Bottom right: Pollo al Mattone (chicken grilled under a brick), a popular Parisi offering.

MARIA EMPANADA

Pop over to Argentina

Lorena Cantarovici loves empanadas—the memories they bring to the surface and the multicultural thread that ties peoples' experiences together. Originally from Argentina, Cantarovici began her journey into restaurant ownership without any experience, being a former banker and accountant, nor being able to speak English.

Starting with the authentic roots of hand-folding the empanadas versus a machine-pressed product, Cantarovici incorporates the art of *repulgue*—folding, sealing, and crimping the empanadas by hand. Each flavor receives a different style to differentiate the fourteen varieties, each carefully crafted using generations-old recipes and local product.

The Rolls Royce of coffee machines is proudly displayed in the Broadway location; only one hundred of them exist in the world and just four in the United States. This particular coffee masterpiece has been blessed by the pope at the Vatican, truly making for "holy coffee." Another unique item available to customers is Quilmes, an Argentinian Beer—99 percent of the Colorado supply is sold through Maria Empanada.

Now fluent in English, Cantarovici showers customers with confidence, having expanded her small garage operation to several storefronts and numerous outlets throughout the city. Crowned the

> Maria Empanadas can be ordered "cocktail sized" for parties or social gatherings twenty-four hours in advance.

Left: Lorena Cantarovici with the blessed coffee machine.

Top right: Spanish chorizo empanadas on display.

Bottom right: Flavors are distinguished through various hand-crimped styles of dough.

"Queen of Empanadas" by Guy Fieri, Cantarovici continues her journey in culinary success. If you're eating a quality empanada in Denver, wherever you may find them, chances are they are Maria Empanada.

1298 S. Broadway
303-934-2221
www.mariaempanada.com
Neighborhood: Platte Park

VESTA

Goddess of hearth

Vesta is a pioneer of what is now known as LoDo or Lower Downtown. Taking up residence in the old building in 1997, then twenty-five-year-old Josh Wolkon energetically built the restaurant of his dreams. Originally Vesta Dipping Grill, the entrepreneur took out a sizable loan, which paid off and gave birth to the Secret Sauce family of unique eateries.

The industrial yet warm space is home to custom metalwork throughout. The location was a warehouse space in an undesirable part of town before its time as a local restaurant.

Secret Sauce encourages a healthy work/life balance, even going so far as to incorporate a Healthy Living Week, supporting staff to hang out without alcohol and offering Healthy Living Week cleanse and gym membership discounts at local Corepower and Orange Theory gyms.

1822 Blake St.
303-296-1970
www.vestadenver.com
Neighborhood: LoDo

"I got into the business because I love throwing parties."
–Owner Josh Wolkon

Top: Interior of Vesta.

Bottom left: The Full Monty charcuterie board.

Bottom right: Day boat diver scallops.

DEPARTURE

Wheels up in Cherry Creek North

Located in the boutique Cherry Creek North Halcyon Hotel, Departure Restaurant and Lounge brings hip Pan-Asian cuisine to Cherry Creek. *Top Chef* runner-up Gregory Gourdet brings his signature dishes from his original outpost in Portland, Oregon, featuring dim sum, kushiyaki, noodles, and more in a contemporary setting with an air-travel motif.

"Departure will allow diners to escape on a global adventure" is a suitable tag line for this modern Pan-Asian restaurant with the centerpiece being the floating bar with a modern and whimsical airplane tail. The large and contemporary space features aerial maps that serve as art. Take a peek at the restaurant's shoji room with its x-rayed suitcase art installation. The space was designed by Skylab Architecture and transports the diner to the feel of an airport terminal a la *The Jetsons*.

Gourdet is the culinary director of Departure Restaurant, with locations in Portland and Cherry Creek. Interestingly, he was a premed student when he discovered his passion for cooking. He found his appetite when he made the jump from medicine to menu planning as he secured a prestigious internship with one of the Jean-Georges restaurants, eventually working his way up to a sous chef position. He honed his craft incorporating Asian cuisine while he was working at Restaurant 66, a modern Chinese establishment.

Check out the speakeasy in the bowels of the hotel if you can find the number to text for a reservation for the exclusive spot.

Left: Fried whole striped bass with mango salad and cashews.

Right: Aerial photography–inspired artwork in Departure's dining room.

Executive chef Khamla Vongsakoun brings more than a decade of experience to Departure Denver. He embraces street fare, sushi, and Pan-Asian cuisine on his menus. Growing up in Colorado, Vongsakoun's career took off in 1997 when he moved to Las Vegas. He conquered Asian cooking working as the sous chef for Buddakan, a contemporary restaurant in Philadelphia. He then moved on to become executive chef at Michael Schulson's Sampan. There he garnered a spot in *Bon Appetit*'s Top 6 Best New Modern Asian Restaurants in 2011. He went from Sampan to work as executive chef at Kittichai, a modern Thai restaurant at the 60 Thompson Hotel in SoHo. Following Kittichai, Vongsakoun honed his culinary cookery at Chelsea's Tao Downtown.

249 Columbine St.
720-772-5020
www.departuredenver.com
Neighborhood: Cherry Creek

17

CRIMSON ROOM

Basement beats

Larimer Street was a hotbed of activity in Denver's early days—horses paraded up the dusty main street while music from saloons and beer halls floated through the thick city air. A post office, bank, and bookstore also lined the street and became the hub of the city. After the silver crash in 1893, Larimer Street waned as the crown jewel of the city, with more than fifty saloons and one-third of Denver's gambling houses opening and catering to out-of-work miners and ranchers.

With the passing of statewide prohibition in 1916, Larimer Street had to get creative to survive. The brothels and saloons cleaned up their act for squeaky-clean facades, albeit sometimes surreptitious speakeasies were hidden away in Denver's playful part of town. Gahan's Saloon was one of the first tenants of the Miller Building, an impressive red brick and rose sandstone corner building overlooking the mountains beyond. A popular watering hole and poker hall for politicians, police, and reporters, the multistory structure was a far cry from Denver's first house, a sixteen-by-twenty-foot cabin erected by General William Larimer in 1858. Becoming Gahan's "Soft Drink Parlor" in 1916, Denver's hottest speakeasy was run out of the basement.

Through World War I and World War II, Larimer Street continued to be Denver's skid row. Voters took action in 1967 to demolish the historic area and an additional thirty blocks of downtown Denver. Preservationist Dana Crawford and a group of

> Adaptive reuse of Denver's Larimer Square has been studied for similar situations around the country.

Left: Bartenders perform crowd-pleasing cocktail creation at the Crimson Room.

Right: Charcuterie board with a selection of dry-cured meats, toasted ciabatta, and mustards.

investors stepped in to prevent the demolition of what is now one of the hottest spots in the city for dining and retailers—the 1400 block of Larimer St, affectionately known as Larimer Square. After prohibition was lifted, Gahan's operated the spot as a restaurant, the first of many iterations of restaurants and bars, even a yacht club–themed bar and then nightclubs in the 1990s. Reverting back to its original calling, the speakeasy-esque space is now home to the Crimson Room, which is owner Brian Sifferman's second location on Larimer Street, the other being a popular champagne bar, Corridor 44. The concept was born as a late-night, after-dinner spot to go for an exclusive experience in the city. Libations are served at the bar or from the tableside bar cart, and live jazz and blues fill the space as a luxury lounge. Velvet banquettes, Swarovski pendant lights, crimson accents, and gleaming gold metalwork make for a much higher brow experience than the humble beginnings of Larimer, a small wooden cabin alongside Cherry Creek.

1403 Larimer St.
720-639-6987
www.crimsonroombardenver.com
Neighborhood: LoDo

PEAKS LOUNGE

Mile-high views

With unparalleled views of the Rocky Mountains from this dining location in the Hyatt Regency Denver, Peaks Lounge may inspire a refrain akin to "America the Beautiful" to be written. Indeed, Pikes Peak, which inspired lyricist Katherine Lee Bates to write "purple mountains majesty," can be seen from the corner of the floor-to-ceiling windows, and the famed Mount Evans is dead ahead from this vantage point high above the city below.

The other direction offers an extensive view of the 16th Street Mall and the Daniels & Fisher Clocktower—a perfect vantage point to witness Fourth of July fireworks, sparkling holiday lights, or fresh spring flowers in bloom. The vistas change with the seasons from this twenty-seventh-floor viewpoint.

Built atop the previous location of St. Mary's Academy, which was founded in 1864 and then moved next door to Molly Brown's House in 1911 (one year before the fateful sinking of the *Titanic* and the inescapable rise to stardom of the "unsinkable Molly Brown"), the Hyatt Regency at Colorado Convention Center was opened on the spot in 2005. Overlooking 14th Street, Peaks Lounge offers a stunning panorama that is forever preserved thanks to a city ordinance that prohibits construction of further high-rises west of the street.

Whether taking in the city or mountain views, sunset from Peaks Lounge is not to be missed. Diners can enjoy local, seasonal fare,

Street-level restaurant Former Saint also pays homage to St. Mary's Academy history.

Above left: Views of the Front Range from Peaks Lounge. Image courtesy of Hyatt Regency Denver.

Above right: Street corn bruschetta with avocado, fry bread, queso fresco, and ancho crema.

Left: Red velvet ice cream sandwich with red velvet chocolate chip cookies, cream cheese gelato, and amaretto chocolate sauce.

a playful cocktail menu, and well-paired small plates while guests can watch vibrant sunsets from the bar area or stormy thunderheads rolling over the Rocky Mountains from fireplace seating all in the cozy comfort of Peaks Lounge.

650 15th St.
303-436-1234
denverregency.hyatt.com
Neighborhood: Downtown

ROSENBERG'S BAGELS & DELICATESSEN

Munchin' with the mensch

Having grown up in the suburbs of New York City, Joshua Pollack is no stranger to the esteemed deli establishments of the East Coast. He attended the University of Colorado Boulder to pursue his interest in business, and his journey into restaurant ownership has turned out to be a significant part of the Denver culinary culture as a whole.

After a stint in event production and other ventures, Pollack returned to school to pursue a degree in business. Following a business plan for Rosenberg's—named after his mother, Karen Rosenberg Pollack—the plan won second place in a university competition, providing him with the funds to begin his vision.

With the restaurant being focused on two of Pollack's loves—food and family—he continued to build his business. After winning a grant to revitalize the then struggling Welton Street corridor, retail occupancy in the now popular area went from 50 percent to 90 percent in two years. A member of the Chef's Collaborative, Pollack focuses on supporting local farmers, educating diners, and promoting sustainable cuisine.

Pollack uses a system to re-create New York water, which is higher in mineral content than Denver water, to produce his bagels.

Left: The Jersey Boy, an egg bagel with double-stack Taylor ham, a fried egg, American cheese, and ketchup.

Top right: Ronnie's Favorite, a bagel sandwich with dill cream cheese, Scottish smoked salmon, whitefish salad, and cucumbers.

Bottom right: Rosenberg's Bagels brings New York–style bagels to the Mile High City.

In 2016, Rosenberg's Bagels was displaced by a fire in the upstairs apartment. Instead of sitting around waiting for the shop to reopen, Pollack and his team hosted a variety of pop-ups and participated in more than a thousand hours of volunteer work. "We're passionate about food and people who share in the community. That's what Rosenberg's is all about," he says.

725 E. 26th Ave.
720-440-9880
www.rosenbergsbagels.com
Neighborhood: Five Points

HIVE

Buzzin' Botanic Gardens

The Denver Botanic Gardens are open to visitors year-round with a wide variety of flora to admire in the extensive facility. Founded in 1951, the intentionally crafted twenty-four acres of gardens incorporate both native plants as well as tropical varietals found in the conservatory.

Previously home to the Monet Café, appropriately located off the water lily pond, Hive Garden Bistro opened in 2014. Overlooking the pond and Le Potager Garden, the shaded deck and dining area are home to seasonal fare, with fresh-picked ingredients incorporated when possible.

1007 York St.
720-865-3500
www.denverbotanicgardens.org
Neighborhood: Cheesman Park

Annual summer concerts and theater are performed in the Denver Botanic Gardens' sunken amphitheater.

Top left: Ingredients from the nearby garden are used as often as possible for a true farm-to-table experience.

Top right: A shaded dining area is a prime place to enjoy fare from Hive.

Bottom left: Poached pear and roasted corn salad with Atlantic salmon.

Bottom right: Overlooking the lily ponds, the dining spot transforms throughout the year with different blooms.

SAUCY NOODLE

If you don't like garlic, go home!

Former big band leader Sam Badis had an eye for Denver business. Playing the piano in establishments around the city, he would eventually buy many of them as an enterprising entrepreneur. The Saucy Noodle was originally founded by Jim Sano in the Bonnie Brae neighborhood, but Sano sold the restaurant in 1964 to his then pianist Badis to get out of a gambling debt. Happy to be free of the restaurant, Sano left to start a new enterprise.

Upon making the dishes and sauces provided in the recipe book left by Sano, Badis and his wife couldn't understand why nothing tasted as it did for the years they had been patronizing the restaurant. Dishwasher Lillian explained that Sano had left them a fake book. His plan all along was to unload the restaurant to pay off the debt and then return later to repurchase what he expected to be a failing business. But there was one thing that Sano didn't take into account: Lillian or "Lil" knew how to make all the recipes from memory. "Would you like me to show you how?" was a phrase that changed the historical trajectory of the restaurant.

Lil became the kitchen manager of what became a successful restaurant, and she remained a part of the family until her passing. In its early years, the Saucy Noodle was one of only two restaurants

Roman chef Francesco Leonardi is credited with first incorporating red sauce with pasta in a 1790 cookbook titled *L'Apicio Moderno*.

Left: Antique artwork collected by Badis adorns the walls at the Saucy Noodle.

Right: Just like mamma used to make: the Margherita-style pizza combines olive oil, diced tomatoes, mozzarella, and fresh basil.

to have a pizza delivery menu, and two full-time delivery drivers serviced the Denver area with delicious pizza pies. A grandson of one of those drivers currently works at the restaurant. Antiques collected by Badis when he was traveling can be found throughout the restaurant, which is owned and managed by his granddaughter Erin Markham. A family business, Erin and her husband, Nathan, continue serving many of the original recipes to hungry customers. Their daughter has also been seen working as a hostess, answering the phone for orders, and waiting tables in some capacity since she was ten.

727 S. University Blvd.
303-733-6977
www.saucynoodle.com
Neighborhood: Bonnie Brae

ADRIFT TIKI BAR & GRILL

Island style

Many locals will say, "The one thing Colorado is missing is the ocean," which is completely true. Adrift Tiki Bar & Grill brings a little island paradise to the Mile High City. Complete with tiki bar, vibrant floral arrangements, tiki statues, and wooden totems, guests feel as if they are in a South Pacific fantasy. Tropical dishes pepper the menu, pots of poke are served in a dreamlike cloud of smoke, and umbrella drinks are poured behind the bar. A back patio is popular on summer nights, and guests are whisked away to tropical paradise steps from South Broadway's bustling street beyond.

Besides fun tropical fare, Adrift is dedicated to bringing positive change to the world through its Mana Immersion Fund—an assistance fund for humanitarians focusing on medical, dental, construction, and hunger relief work. Believing in the spirit of *ohana* (Hawaiian for family), a portion of all profits from the restaurant go

> Maori mythology refers to Tiki as the first man, and carved wooden totems represent a variety of Polynesian gods.

Left: Tiki god statues and totems overlook diners enjoying an island paradise.
Right: Confit chicken wings with sweet chili sambal sauce and sweet soy sauce.

toward the fund, which helps recipients to immerse themselves in projects all across the globe.

A remnant of the vibrant Tiki scene between the 1960s and 1980s in Denver, Adrift is going strong with its 2,200 square feet of rum-infused enjoyment. Whether you are sipping on a mai tai or enjoying hula lessons every Saturday in the summer, Adrift is a truly unique restaurant in the city.

218 S. Broadway
303-778-8454
www.adriftbar.com
Neighborhood: Baker

GOZO

SoBo swine

Crackling oak can be heard igniting in the open flame oven, and reclaimed decorator wood warms the interior look and feel for this Mediterranean-inspired eatery. Drawing from Spanish and Italian influences, this Baker neighborhood space imbues a welcoming and comforting environment, with food that will knock you out of your chair.

Simple, elegant, and clean describes both the food and the decor. Refined simplicity finds its way throughout the GOZO experience. The laid-back and comfortable atmosphere is reminiscent of the inclusive neighborhood ambiance of the Maltese archipelago.

Owner Frank Jolley began collecting antique menus and speakers, which are now on display at the restaurant, adding to the charm of this spot, which opened in 2013.

30 S. Broadway
720-638-1462
www.gozodenver.com
Neighborhood: Baker

Down the street from the historic Mayan Theatre, GOZO is located on a walkable street that's perfect for dinner and a movie.

Top: Grilled Spanish octopus served with braised potato, pickled onion, and salsa verde.

Bottom left: The countertop near the wood-fired oven is a perfect vantage point to see the chefs at work.

Bottom right: The asparagus pizza is made with "00" flour and wood-fired at eight hundred degrees.

STEUBEN'S ARVADA

Retro replica

The retro vibe from the '40s and '50s can be felt throughout Steuben's Arvada location. The second location to grace the Denver scene, the Arvada site is an authentic nod to the original Boston Steuben's started by owner Josh Wolkon's great-uncles, Max and Joe, in 1945.

Home to American regional classics, the deli cold cuts, lobster rolls, green chili cheeseburger, and house-made desserts harken back to the era. Launching a food truck in 2009, Steuben's was one of the first to help actualize the food truck scene in Denver, and two trucks are still out and about bringing Steuben's food to eager eaters at events throughout the city.

Housed in a renovated twenty-five-year-old diner, Steuben's is located near historic Olde Town, a perfect place for this retro concept.

7355 Ralston Rd.
303-830-0096
www.steubens.com
Neighborhood: Arvada

"What nicer thing to do for somebody than to make them breakfast."   –banner above dining room at Steuben's

Top left: Cubano with pork shoulder, ham, Swiss cheese, pickles, and dijonaise in a pressed bolillo roll.

Bottom left: Steubie Snacks (pieces of braised pork shoulder that have been deep fried and dredged in powdered sugar) are a popular appetizer.

Top right: Monte Cristo with ham, turkey, and Swiss and American cheese, battered and deep fried, topped with powdered sugar, and served with a side of house-made raspberry preserves.

Center right: The diner-style decor and feel harkens back to a bygone era.

Bottom right: Steuben's Arvada exterior is a beacon for lovers of comfort food.

AD HOMINEM

Negative way to argue, positive way to cook

Walking the streets of Greece, legend has it that Diogenes carried a lamp during the day, shining the bright light into passersby's faces looking for an honest man. Credited with being one of the founders of the philosophy of cynicism, his theory was that virtue is better revealed in action than in theory. The restaurant steers clear of the traditional definition of ad hominem—an argument directed against a person rather than the position he is maintaining—and instead focuses on the lesser-known meaning of "relating to a particular person." Just inside the entrance is an oversized art piece emblazoned with the words "ad ho·mi·nem— empathic, honest, thoughtful, disciplined, natural, a restaurant for the people of Denver."

Chef Chris Martinez brings that light and thought to his food and catered experience for guests of Ad Hominem. Crafting "humbly pretentious" food, Martinez's aim is to bring accessible fine dining to downtown. Pushing the guest to try something new and to trust the chef, the entire team is eager for diners to ask questions, learn about the food they are preparing, and take the education with them. Much like Diogenes's quest for an honest man, Martinez's light brings transparency to his offerings, as he often gives out recipes and informs guests of where ingredients are sourced. In a literal transparency, a farm by Rebel Farm is a showpiece in the dining room, with microgreens, kale, and other seasonal vegetables

> "We want guests to taste the best food they've ever tasted– every day."   –Chris Martinez

Left: Bouillabaisse, a shellfish and seafood medley featuring fennel and lemongrass in a tomato broth, accompanied by a piece of grilled bread slathered in garlic aioli.

Right: Trio of desserts at Ad Hominem.

growing right in front of guests and harvested minutes before landing on beautifully constructed plates.

"We have to prove ourselves on a daily basis," Chef Martinez explains. Even after his ten years of executive chef training, the art is consumed as soon as it is created.

Staffed by a young group of professionals with credits at some of the most prestigious restaurants in Denver, Ad Hominem almost feels like a fine-dining underground, bucking conventional approaches and disrupting the food scene both in the front and back of the house. Creative staff members have contributed their talents to make a remarkable space. The Binchotan charcoal used in cooking the food has also been crafted into the bar by some of the chefs, and they've used reclaimed wood in wall accents and in a service station.

43 W. 9th Ave.
303-454-0000
www.adhominemdenver.com
Neighborhood: Lincoln Park

LITTLE MAN ICE CREAM

I scream, you scream

You can't miss the twenty-eight-foot-tall, fourteen-thousand-pound milk cream can in Lower Highlands that is Little Man Ice Cream. Opened on the Fourth of July 2008, this neighborhood hot spot takes on the time-honored tradition of a local ice cream shop. Handmade small-batch ice cream in six-gallon batches includes such flavors as salted Oreo, French toast, banana pudding, and coconut almond.

Little Man Ice Cream sits on the parking lot of the Oliver Mortuary building, which has since been converted into a restaurant, and the cobblestone courtyard is a hotbed of activity in the summer months. Every night of the week the community gathers for everything from swing dancing on Saturdays and projected movies on Fridays to bingo on Thursdays and live jazz on Wednesdays, all while enjoying rich and creamy ice cream.

The Scoop for Scoop program, started by owner Paul Tamburello on day one, offers a scoop of rice and beans to a third-world country for every scoop of ice cream sold at Little Man Ice Cream. So far, more than three million scoops of food have been donated to communities in need across the globe.

Inspired by the nostalgia of the great American road trip era of the 1920s to the 1950s, Little Man was named after Tamburello's

Little Man Ice Cream is also used in the popular ice cream sandwiches available at the stand.

Left: Little Man Ice Cream's landmark milk cream can.

Right: Unique flavors such as Salted Oreo, 16th St. Chocolate, Raspberry Love, and Salted Caramel PB Cup are all delicious.

father, who was nicknamed Little Man. While small in stature, Peter Tamburello's heart was as big as the towering cream can. Paul named the company in his honor to continue the family legacy of giving back to the community and making a positive difference.

2620 16th St.
303-455-3811
www.littlemanicecream.com
Neighborhood: LoHi

BLACKBELLY

Boulder butcher

Founded as a boutique catering company in 2011, Blackbelly expanded in 2014, opening its doors as a high-end, meat-focused restaurant. Working with ranchers who apply all-natural, humane standards in raising and slaughtering their animals, the popular establishment is a staple of Boulder and beyond for choice cuts of meat.

The whole animal butchery program is a ballet of blades; swift cuts utilize each animal in its entirety, leaving no waste behind. The restaurant is named after the heritage breed of Blackbelly lamb. In addition to its lamb, Blackbelly is just as synonymous with its outstanding beef, which is dry aged in-house for thirty to sixty days on average. Cuts offered include everything from popular tenderloins and rib eyes to lesser-known but just as tasty butcher's cuts, such as bavettes and Denver steaks. Furthermore, Blackbelly is the only independent restaurant in Boulder County licensed to make and sell its own house-cured meats. All the ranches from which Blackbelly's meat is sourced are local, ranging from a few miles up the road, to a few hours drive from the restaurant. The terroir on which the animals graze, what they eat, and the quality of their lives is very important and is ultimately reflected in the flavors of the meat.

Originally farming and raising the livestock himself, Chef Hosea Rosenberg began to source his product from trusted partners to better focus on the restaurant business. A typical week on the

Blackbelly sells more than five thousand pounds of lamb per year.

Left: Chef Hosea Rosenberg at the butcher counter.

Right: Seasonal ingredients, such as these squash blossoms, are incorporated into Blackbelly's fare.

butcher block includes the breakdown of about two lambs, two half pigs, and half a cow. Head butcher Nate Singer (the first employee of Blackbelly) orchestrates the fabrication of all the meat, working with the chefs to determine whether it will be used for the butcher shop, market, restaurant, or catering.

The open kitchen in the restaurant is an important aspect of the Blackbelly dining experience to Rosenberg, adding to the sense of transparency in both the butcher shop and restaurant alike. "We want to show how the food is handled and treated," he explains. Cooks chat amiably with guests about where the ingredients are from and why they are used in certain dishes, with quick trips to cut fresh herbs and flowers grown just outside to finish off their plates.

1606 Conestoga St., #3
303-247-1000
www.blackbelly.com
Neighborhood: Boulder

SUMMIT

Mountain races inspire space and sustenance

Racing around perilous blind turns and kicking up dust from spinning tires, the nail-biting Race to the Clouds was all performed with the magnificent Pikes Peak region acting as a backdrop. The annual invitational automobile and motorcycle climb was started in 1916 and continues to influence the area today, down to the very architecture that Summit restaurant calls home.

A group of former competitors, race officials, crew members, and race enthusiasts came together in 1989 to preserve the history of the Race to the Clouds. Affectionately known as the "Over the Hill Gang," they organize the digital archive and meet monthly to swap stories and work on projects dedicated to continuing the story of the race.

The need for speed is found within Summit restaurant as well. Adam D. Tihany's design pays homage to the summit finish line of the races, incorporating various abstracted elements of cars, engines, and the grandeur of the mountains into the design of the space. Steel Y-beams greet guests at the facade, with a towering fourteen-foot cylindrical wine turret slowly rotating behind the bar upon entering. The curved grace of the floorplan is as elegant as the vintage race cars that have traversed the mountain in the transportation museum next door, with abstracted design elements, such as car grills and carburetors, elegantly designed into banquette backsplashes and chandeliers.

"Everything was created to give the illusion of speed and movement," explains Tihany. "It is meant to convey the feeling

Rea Lentz won the first Race to the Clouds in 1916 using a homemade car.

40

Left: Summit's dining room.
Right: Cucumber hamachi.

that you are sitting in a car, and everything is going by very quickly. The carpet simulates the movement of car gears, the ceiling in the main restaurant is designed like a racetrack, and I conceived the wine turret, complete with moving racks, to suggest the gears of a race car. However, none of these details are evident. They are only suggestions, hints, and metaphors."

Produce from Broadmoor Farms, meats from Corner Post Ranch (a herd raised on land leased from Audubon Rockies), and tortillas from Raquelitas bring locally sourced ingredients to the restaurant's American contemporary regional cuisine for a twist as curvy as the mountain road to the top.

19 Lake Circle
719-577-5896
www.broadmoor.com/dining/summit
Neighborhood: Colorado Springs

CIVIC CENTER EATS FOOD TRUCKS

Rotating moveable feast

Since 2005 food trucks have been gathering at Civic Center Park for the annual Civic Center EATS. Produced by the Civic Center Conservancy, more than eighty diverse vendors now gather Tuesdays, Wednesdays, and Thursdays from 11:00 a.m. to 2:00 p.m., May through November.

Over a century old, Civic Center Park is a jewel of the city. The conservancy aims to restore, maintain, and activate the space, which includes fountains, sculptures, an amphitheater, and sprawling flower beds. Hungry diners can select from approximately twenty-five options per day. Many of the brick-and-mortar restaurants in Denver began as food trucks and part of this movement.

The food trucks offer something for everyone, including a spicy chicken stew in berbere with injera (a traditional Ethiopian cuisine found at Saba's Ethiopian Food truck) and a Monterey Pepper Jack Hatch green chili grilled cheese on sourdough brioche from Snack Shack's truck. The diversity found in such a small footprint exposes diners to foods they might not have tried before or old favorites brought right to the heart of the city and nearby places of work.

101 W. 14th Ave.
civiccenterconservancy.org/event-civic-center-eats-2015_88.html
Neighborhood: Civic Center

Denver's food truck industry has tripled since 2014.

WeChef Asian nachos: crispy fried wonton chips with marinated steak, homemade slaw, and cilantro, smothered in sweet soy and Sriracha mayo and topped with toasted sesame seeds.

ZAIDY'S DELI CHERRY CREEK

Bring your bubbe

This New York–style deli opened in 1992 before the Cherry Creek neighborhood saw towering apartment complexes and mega malls. Zaidy's is home to by-the-slice or whole baked goods, chicken matzo ball soup, and a famed potato latke sandwich with corned beef, pastrami, or brisket served between two latkes. The old-world recipes paired with the communal atmosphere make for a special spot in Cherry Creek.

Zaidy is the Yiddish word for grandfather, and Zaidy's delights in old-world food, piling high thin-cut meats for their Reuben and slicing generous servings of cake. The decor features antique photos of the city and family members. Now dwarfed by surrounding buildings, the small but mighty storefront is a beacon to those seeking good company and comfort food.

Cakes line the counters and fill the cases alongside deli meats and cheeses. Using family recipes, owner Gerard Rudofsky oversees the 150-seat restaurant that is typically packed with guests. Whether reading newspapers at the counter, meeting with friends or weekly

> Matzo in matzo ball soup is part of the traditional Passover meal and represents the unleavened bread eaten by the Jews fleeing Egypt.

Left: Tasty from-scratch treats on display at Zaidy's.

Right: Zaidy's Reuben is served with a choice of corned beef, pastrami, or turkey with Swiss cheese, sauerkraut, and Russian dressing.

social groups at a table, or stopping by for the mouthwatering corned beef hash, visitors to the spot feel like family and are welcomed as such.

121 Adams St.
303-333-5336
www.zaidysdeli.com
Neighborhood: Cherry Creek

BEAST + BOTTLE

Sibling sensation on 17th

A crispy pig's head is served on the table next to us. Apparently, you have to preorder such an experience, and it is best to bring hungry friends. Beast + Bottle, brainchild of siblings Paul Reilly and Aileen Reilly, is a farm-focused, snout-to-tail experience.

Opened in 2013, the pair previously ran Encore on Colfax, where Paul was the executive chef after helping open Mirepoix in 2004. The bustling patio of B+B is a common site on 17th Street, a popular culinary destination in Uptown. Curated wine lists and rotating, ever-fresh menu offerings with artful plating make for a unique experience, even within the Denver dining scene. Themed dinners bring foodie fans and rockers alike, with menus in honor of noted names, such as Led Zeppelin, the Beatles, and the Rolling Stones.

719 E. 17th Ave.
303-623-3223
www.beastandbottle.com
Neighborhood: Uptown

Top left: Summer salad with garden vegetables.

Top right: Scotch What Happens, one of many cleverly named drinks on the cocktail menu.

Bottom: Beast + Bottle's beautifully designed space is intimate and sophisticated.

POSTINO LOHI

Arizona post office to Denver book bindery

Postino has a creative way of making repurposed locations really pop. Italian for "postman," Postino takes its name from its first location, a 1940s brick post office in Phoenix, Arizona.

Located in the historic Denver Bookbinding Company building, Postino offers a breathtaking view of the city from its eight-hundred-square-foot patio. Not forgetting its roots, the entire entryway wall is covered in a mosaic of old books, careful not to erase what made LoHi so special to begin with. Closed in 2013, the bindery had been in operation as a warehouse for fifty-three years before being converted to the chic restaurant.

Oversized bruschettas are a staple of the restaurant, which is primarily a wine bar with an extensive collection. Sandwiches, salads, and charcuterie boards are served, and local beers can be found on tap. The energetic patio is full for lunch and dinner during the summer, and the signature garage door windows bring light to the previously cavernous and dark warehouse space.

2715 17th St.
303-433-6363
www.postinowinecafe.com
Neighborhood: LoHi

Denver Bookbinding Company is still in operation today at another location and has been in business since 1929.

Top: A wall of books pays homage to the previous use of the space.

Center left: Large bruschetta offerings are enough for a meal or to share with friends.

Bottom left: Paninis pair well with wine, either in the dining room or on the patio.

Right: An extensive selection of Colorado wines can be enjoyed alongside a meat and cheese tray.

MERCANTILE

Union Station marvel

Mercantile is a culmination of Chef Alex Seidel's two restaurant ventures, Fruition Restaurant and Fruition Farms. Many restaurants talk about farm to table, but Chef Seidel purchased a small farm outside Denver in 2009 and named it Fruition Farms, where they raise heritage breed pigs, Italian honeybees, fresh fruits, and vegetables. He has his own sheep's milk creamery, the first of its kind in Colorado. Fruition Farms, located south of Larkspur, Colorado, recently sold its herd of East Friesian sheep but still works with the new owners to source the milk product.

Seidel was always in search of great sheep's milk cheese for his restaurant and could not find it. Unlike Spain, which is known for its sheep's milk cheese, such as Manchego, the United States had very few options. Since the logical next step in his quest for superior product was to start a farm, Seidel rolled up his white chef's coat sleeves and got to it.

Seidel began his culinary career at fourteen, serving as a sous chef at a local, well-known restaurant. Now he has several *Food & Wine* Best Chef titles under his belt, as his career has taken him from Denver to Pebble Beach. He worked at Hubert Keller's Club at the Pebble Beach Resort and then at the celebrated Vail Valley restaurant, Sweet Basil. He returned to Denver and worked at Mizuna and then launched his own Fruition Restaurant.

Ten-acre Fruition Farms is home to dairy production, Large Black pork, vegetable gardens, and fruit trees to supply the Fruition family restaurants.

Left: A cheese and baked-goods counter adjacent to spice racks and provisions.
Right: This scallop dish is as much a feast for the eyes as the appetite.

Mercantile is the largest restaurant in Denver's 1894 Union Station train depot. The five-thousand-square-foot space includes an artisanal market, state-of-the-art barista station, chef's counter, wine library, and open kitchen. Denver's Union Station train depot houses Mercantile Dining and Provision and the Crawford Hotel, with the reimagined Terminal Bar, which has four beehives on the rooftop that provide honey for many of the dessert items found in the on-site restaurants. Mercantile, a European-style market and counter, is a great place to not only have a memorable meal but also to pick up provisions, such as spices and rubs, fresh-baked pastries, and cheeses from Fruition Farms.

1701 Wynkoop St., #155
720-460-3733
www.mercantiledenver.com
Neighborhood: LoDo

RHEIN HAUS

See ya lederhosen

Under ornate chandeliers imported from Austria, beers and brats are served at Rhein Haus. A popular haunt for World Cup enthusiasts, the restaurant welcomes world culture in the LoDo location overlooking Market Street through the building's original historic windowpanes.

Rhein Haus, which originally hails from Seattle and is co-owned by former Denverites, is a beloved independent, Bavarian-inspired restaurant, which opened in 2015 in Denver's LoDo neighborhood. A unique space featuring two stories of inspired decor sourced from around the world, Rhein Haus offers four indoor bocce ball courts and two separate bars. The restaurant serves house-made sausages and pretzels as well as a selection of salads, sandwiches, entrées, and a variety of German, Belgian, and American beers, with a heavy focus on lagers.

Rhein Haus occupies two full stories and six thousand square feet of space that was occupied by Old Chicago Pizza & Taproom's Denver flagship location from 1992 to 2014.

1415 Market St.
303-800-2652
www.rheinhausdenver.com
Neighborhood: LoDo

The ornate upstairs fireplace was imported from northern France to its Colorado home.

Top left: Diners enjoy Bavaria-inspired cuisine beneath decor sourced from around the world.

Top right: Rhein Haus offers a large selection of house-made gourmet sausages.

Bottom left: Bocce is the Italian version of boules, a collective term for games in which bigger balls are thrown as close as possible to a smaller, target ball. Boules is played throughout Germany and Austria, as well as the rest of Europe.

Bottom right: Giant pretzels, a Rhein Haus staple, are baked from scratch daily and served with house-made sauces.

CASA BONITA

Delighting audiences for more than forty years

As a child growing up in Denver, celebrating a birthday at Casa Bonita is almost a rite of passage. The pink stucco building is tucked away in a strip mall located just off America's longest commercial street, Colfax Avenue; blink and you miss it. The eatery is virtually unchanged since its opening in 1974.

The whimsical dining experience includes a tropical rain forest with faux palm trees, volcanic rocks, gunfights, gorillas, and cliff divers. Diners can experience the backsplash beside a thirty-foot waterfall that resembles the cliffs of Acapulco, as divers gracefully enter the fourteen-foot-deep pool below.

Casa Bonita boasts a 250-seat theater and 52,000 square feet of dining and entertainment space, and it seats more than a thousand guests. The fountain in the restaurant was shipped in pieces from Mexico, and the dome is covered with 22-karat gold leaf and features a statue of Cuauhtémoc, the last Aztec emperor.

The restaurant is considered one of America's top roadside attractions and has been delighting audiences with its quirky collection of kitsch—strolling mariachi bands, puppet shows, and villain Black Bart's secret cave hideout—gratifying children and forging Colorado memories that will last a lifetime.

6715 W. Colfax Ave.
303-232-5115
www.casabonitadenver.com
Neighborhood: West Colfax

The first Casa Bonita was opened in 1968 in Oklahoma City.

Top: A thirty-foot waterfall is the centerpiece of Casa Bonita's dining space.

Bottom left: The unmistakable entrance to Casa Bonita.

Bottom right: Cavern-inspired booths transport guests to another country.

BASTA

Enough!

Hard-to-find eateries are sometimes the best-hidden treasures of all. Basta, or "enough" in Italian, is nestled within an apartment complex, where the boutique restaurant churns out some serious cuisine.

Specialty cut and cured wood is stacked in the restaurant, waiting to bake bread (1,000°), roast vegetables (500°), and cook pizzas, meats, and fish (1,000°+). "We find using the one oven forces our creativity," says chef/owner Kelly Whitaker. "Basta has really become a lab. We explore a lot of different culinary options."

One successful experiment is the aptly named Campfire Vanilla Ice Cream, with its creamy texture and slightly smoky finish. "We have had many guests reflect on times they have been camping with friends and family," explains Whitaker. The ice cream is created by smoking sugars and vanilla beans, and then churning them with liquid nitrogen. Puffed fish skin chicharron sculpted quickly after a brush with fire and garnished with a black garlic sauce is another fire-infused menu offering, and there's a wood-fired vegetable salad dressing that's created by immersing a hot coal in olive oil and infusing it for twenty-four hours in the oven.

As a cofounder of the Noble Grain Alliance, Whitaker seeks to return to using local heritage grains in everything from farming to

Two hundred pounds of house-milled flour are used every month at Basta.

Left: Baked piada bread comes fresh and crispy from the oven.
Right: The chef's table overlooks a wood-fueled oven and prep area.

home kitchens, as opposed to using commodity wheat grown and milled in bulk. By nurturing the production of spelt, White Sonora, and emmer, Whitaker aims to further the voice of chefs choosing their own foods and sources beyond locally grown.

3601 Arapahoe Ave.
303-997-8775
www.bastaboulder.com
Neighborhood: Boulder

THE FAMILY JONES

We are family

The relationship between distiller, chef, bartender, and guest can be complicated, just like any family dynamic. Playfully coining the term "bitchen" (a hybrid of the words "bar" and "kitchen"), the goal of the distillery and tasting room is to break down the barriers between front-of-house operations and back-of-house kitchen and distillery.

Upon entering the space, guests will notice the centerpiece of it all: the towering German copper still that is just as architecturally stunning as it is practical. Small plates pair with craft-distilled options, such as vodka, gin, bourbon, whiskey, rum, crème de violet, and a Colorado pine amaretto. A virtual who's who of the Denver culinary scene comes together to create the family, with backgrounds from well-known brands, such as Spring 44, Linger, and Williams & Graham.

The last use of the space was a tattoo parlor, but the occupants before that were family based as well. Mancinelli's Market was a family-owned Italian market that served the LoHi and Sunnyside neighborhoods during the 1980s.

3245 Osage St.
303-481-8185
www.thefamilyjones.co
Neighborhood: LoHi

The menus at the Family Jones are inspired by family photo albums and feature vintage black-and-white photos found in antique shops. The photos rotate and change regularly.

Top left: Food pairs with house-made spirits for a fine-dining experience with a neighborhood feel.

Bottom left: The family of spirits at the Family Jones includes rum, gin, vodka, bourbon, and rye.

Top right: The copper still can be seen from the dining room, creating a unique space.

Bottom right: Artichoke fondue is a guest favorite.

KEVIN TAYLOR'S OPERA HOUSE

Sing for your supper

Kevin Taylor has opened many successful restaurants, all appealing to those with a sophisticated palette as well as those with a love for the arts. His flagship restaurant, Kevin Taylor's at the Opera House, is a hot ticket before each show at the Denver Performing Arts Complex.

The building was originally the Municipal Auditorium. When it was constructed to host the 1908 Democratic National Convention, it was the largest auditorium in the United States outside Madison Square Garden in New York. In addition to presidential political rallies, the building accommodated theatrical performances, conventions, and even circuses and rodeos.

Thanks to the generous funding of the Caulkins family as well as the city, the space was reborn as the Ellie Caulkins Opera House in 2005. The lyric opera house and its accompanying spaces, which were all part of the original Newton Auditorium campus, are now a vital part of the Denver Performing Arts Complex. Today, it is affectionately known as "The Ellie" and hosts a diverse range of world-renowned performers and assorted entertainment, ranging from colorful comedians and rock concerts to performances by Opera Colorado.

The Denver Center for the Performing Arts is the nation's largest nonprofit theater organization.

Left: Grilled filet mignon with baby carrots, Yukon mousse, pearl onions, and watercress.

Right: Lavender white chocolate mousse with cocoa cake, thyme oat streusel, and *crème fraîche*.

Kevin Taylor's at the Opera House definitely appeals to individuals with a passion for exquisite food and fine theater performances. The beautiful space features romantic lighting, stone-lined walls, colorful artwork from Colorado artist Vance Kirkland, and framed historical theater costumes from performances past. This setting sweeps diners into a night of theatrical performance, starting with the food.

In 1987, at the age of twenty-five, self-taught chef Kevin Taylor opened his first restaurant, serving his unique take on Southwestern cuisine, which became one of the three top-rated restaurants in Denver. He quickly garnered awards and recognition from media outlets all over the country, including *Bon Appetit*, *Restaurant Hospitality*, and *GQ*. "When I cook, the first and foremost thought

Butter-poached lobster with curry-charred cauliflower, roasted beets, and fine herb pistou.

in my mind is that each guest needs to be wowed," says Taylor. "I take perfection seriously and am constantly looking for ways to improve myself as a chef, the food, the ambiance, and setting, and how people feel when they dine in my restaurants."

1345 Champa St.
303-640-1012
www.ktrg.net
Neighborhood: Downtown

Top: The restaurant's walls are adorned with framed historical theater costumes.

Bottom: A piece from famed Colorado artist Vance Kirkland is the centerpiece of the bar. Photo courtesy of Kevin Taylor Restaurant Group.

SHELBY'S BAR & GRILL

Historic building amidst towering skyscrapers

The vast plains of Denver began to be tamed at the end of the nineteenth century and beginning of the twentieth. Originally pasture land, the corner of what is now 18th and Glenarm was a far cry from the glass-and-steel metropolis of today. The Adams Hotel was built in 1901, and next to the hotel a small wooden house was constructed in 1906 by an enterprising and pioneering Denverite.

Shortly after construction of the house, it was converted into the Whitehead Undertaking Parlor. The ghost of John Paul Potter still visits the site, playing tricks such as making ketchup bottles roll, flushing toilets, and moving cans around the kitchen. During the Roaring '20s, the structure was converted into a restaurant and has been an iteration of an eatery ever since. In 1933, Emil Servino opened Emil's Café, which was transformed into Emil's Spaghetti Garden in 1939. Growing in popularity, the restaurant was reimagined as Emil's Famous Spaghetti Café in 1942.

Following the Italian-inspired restaurant, the Pink Lady Lounge opened as a bordello in 1949. A sophisticated system of underground tunnels facilitated secret rendezvous between the Pink Lady Lounge, neighboring houses of ill repute, and local businesses and hotels. In 1956, a rib joint took over the site. Changing hands again in 1979, the current name of Shelby's Bar and Grill finally stuck. It was located next door to the region's first discount liquor retailer, and patrons would travel from as far as Montana to stock

> An oversize postcard mural on the side of the building reads, "Where The Locals Gather."

Above: Menu staples, such as the burrito (in bean, beef, or chicken), one of the best Reuben sandwiches in Denver, and the Shelby burger with black olives, Wisconsin cheddar, and Swiss cheese, keep locals and visitors coming back for more.

Left: An original surrounded by new development, the charm of this restaurant is something special in Denver.

up on alcohol, further driving business to the neighborhood bar and grill.

Named "Denver's Cheers Bar" by *Esquire* magazine, Shelby's serves American and Mexican food. Colorado green chili is smothered over burritos, Reuben sandwiches are devoured by local businesspeople and tourists alike, and the Shelby Burger is lathered in Wisconsin and Swiss cheese and stacked with olives.

519 18th St.
303-295-9597
Neighborhood: Downtown

SNOOZE, AN A.M. EATERY

Breakfast bedlam

I f you're driving around Denver and you see a gathering of people waiting to get into a breakfast restaurant, chances are it's Snooze. This popular restaurant commands a loyal following willing to play cornhole or sip complimentary coffee as they await their favorite Snooze dishes.

Legendary for their pineapple upside-down pancakes, the locally owned and operated restaurant began on Larimer Street in 2006. The retro-accented decor of the 1890s building served as a launching pad for brothers Jon and Adam Schlegel to create their restaurant empire.

With a history of restaurant work, Jon would come home after late-night shifts and hit the snooze button at least three times before heading to work again the next day. But after opening an A.M. eatery of his own with Adam, apparently the early mornings no longer bother him as he bounds from bed.

One percent of all Snooze sales goes back into the local community in in-kind goods or services. Passing out pancakes, volunteering at food banks, and maintaining school gardens are all part of the Snooze corporate environment. Staff help select charities to volunteer at while fulfilling the company mantra: it only takes a moment to make a difference.

Ancient Greeks and Romans regularly enjoyed pancakes sweetened with honey, and the history of the pancake may reach back to the Ice Age.

Left: Retro decor and splashes of color make for a cozy dining space in Denver.

Right: The Bella! Bella! Benny: thin slices of prosciutto, Taleggio cheese, and perfectly poached eggs on toasted ciabatta, topped with cream cheese hollandaise, balsamic glaze, and arugula.

With more than thirty-one locations in four states, the popular Snooze concept continues to grow. Whether enjoying pineapple upside-down pancakes, breakfast pot pie, or the smashed avocado Benny, there's something for everyone at Snooze.

2262 Larimer St.
303-297-0700
www.snoozeeatery.com
Neighborhood: Ballpark

BIKER JIM'S GOURMET DOGS

Hardcore hot dogs

Repo man turned tycoon Jim Pittenger is the real deal. A portrait of Jim on a Harley-Davidson hangs in the Biker Jim's restaurant near Coors Field above a floor where he held a "burn out" with bikes before sealing the concrete. Impressive skid marks set the tone for the distinctive and exotic dogs to be ordered.

After confiscating more than twelve thousand cars as a repossession agent, Pittenger started Biker Jim's from a tricked-out cart on the 16th Street Mall. After expanding to three carts, the Larimer Street location became an actuality eight years after starting his first cart, where lines snaked around the block (some guests actually enjoying rattlesnake-and-pheasant sausages).

Forbes rated Biker Jim's as one of the top ten hot dog restaurants in the country, and Foursquare ranked the restaurant as the nation's fourth-best hot dog haunt. Biker Jim's was also featured on Anthony Bourdain's *No Reservations* and Andrew Zimmerman's *Bizarre Foods*. The unique flavors and meats, such as yak, Alaskan reindeer, buffalo, chicken rosemary, and German veal, have led to more than seven hundred thousand hot dog sales.

2148 Larimer St.
720-746-9355
www.bikerjimsdogs.com
Neighborhood: Ballpark

Colorado Rockies fans can grab a dog before seeing a game at nearby Coors Field.

Top left: Artwork on historic brick in the main dining room.

Top right: Tire marks on the floor from the "burn out" before opening give the space a distinct look.

Bottom: Elk jalapeño cheddar dog with the Conspiracy topper: bleu cheese, bacon red onion marmalade, lemon aioli, and french fried onions.

MORRISON INN

Music on the mind in the foothills

Red Rocks Amphitheatre is a world-renowned stage on which legendary bands, such as the Beatles, the Blues Brothers, and the Grateful Dead, have performed. Nestled in the valley adjacent to Red Rocks is the small mountain town of Morrison. It is comfortably positioned to welcome concertgoers and hungry tourists alike.

Built in the late 1800s, the building that now houses the Morrison Inn has been family owned and operated as a restaurant since 1979. With a hundred-person-plus patio and live music, the historic location continues to welcome diners through its doors. Award-winning margaritas incorporate high-end tequila and house-made sweet and sour (60-oz. oversized glasses are available for those truly looking to imbibe). Pouring more than fifteen thousand gallons of margaritas annually and serving fifty thousand pounds of complimentary chips and salsa, the Inn has come miles from serving only twenty-five meals their first day.

Morrison, a settlement of twenty-five people founded by George Morrison in the 1860s, soon became a popular stopping point for travelers heading west to the mines of South Park. A narrow-gauge railroad was incorporated in 1872 and completed by Governor John Evans, with service to Mt. Morrison for sixty cents round-trip in 1874. The railway ran until 1918 with four round-trips daily.

The Morrison Inn was originally built in 1880 as the Pike & Perry Mercantile. Historic images of iterations of the building over

Your eyes don't deceive you. Mannequin Juan does move as an animatronic addition to the dining room.

Left: Juan waits for hungry patrons at the Morrison Inn.

Right: The Tostada Grande pairs perfectly with an award-winning margarita.

the years are on display in the dining room. Burned in 1919 and repaired, the building became a dance hall under the guidance of Mazie and David O. Gage. Floods devastated the area in 1938, wiping out the railroad bridges and ushering in a new business, the Schneider family drugstore, which operated from 1938 to 1973. After a series of expansions into adjacent properties, the Morrison Inn has become what it is today: a series of dining rooms, a large patio with views of the red rocks landscape, a sunroom, and a bar. Whether strolling the quaint town seeking antiques and listening to the bubbling stream or making your way to a concert at the famed Red Rocks Amphitheatre, the Morrison Inn is still a stop worth making in this historic town.

301 Bear Creek Ave.
303-697-6650
www.morrisoninn.com
Neighborhood: Morrison

FRASCA

Branching out

Only about three hundred Americans per year visit the region of Friuli-Venezia Giulia in the northeast corner of Italy. Bordered by Slovenia and Austria and facing the Adriatic Sea, the region boasts flavors that are complex and unexpected. Frasca Boulder embraces the flavors of this unique locale, with owners Lachlan Mackinnon-Patterson and Bobby Stuckey of the French Laundry fame partnering to launch this innovative concept.

Located in an old grocery store, Frasca continues the culinary roots today. An Italian tradition, frasca was a branch that was placed above doorways indicating to travelers in the neighborhood that meals were to be had within. The branch withered over the season as the frasca came to a close. Master sommelier Stuckey chose the wines of the region for their unique whites along the old Slavic spice routes. Diners are in for a treat, as Frasca is home to hundreds of exceptional varietals, which are paired with food reflective of the area.

Couple Executive Chef Eduardo Valle Lobo and Chef Kelly Jeun used to work in the Friuli-Venezia Giulia restaurant Orsone Ristorante, where they originally met Stuckey and Mackinnon-

Nearby Pearl Street Mall is a four-block pedestrian mall and Boulder's top tourist attraction, perfect for a stroll after dinner.

Top left: A twist on a caprese salad, this dish incorporates a cheese gelato over sliced tomatoes and herbs.

Bottom left: Seasonal ingredients are incorporated into Frasca's fare, such as the plums added to this dish.

Right: Fish topped with squash scales; colorful squash blossoms decorate the dish.

Patterson. An expert in Friulian cooking, they were a perfect fit for the unique Frasca stage.

1738 Pearl St.
303-442-6966
www.frascafoodandwine.com
Neighborhood: Boulder

COOHILLS

Waterfront dining

As the only restaurant on the water in Denver, Coohills Restaurant and Bar is reminiscent of what you might find in European river towns.

Coohills specializes in handmade, carefully crafted French cuisine created from local, organic, and farm-fresh ingredients. Located in the urban Lower Downtown, Coohills has a modern indoor restaurant and bar and an outdoor terrace. Adjacent to the restaurant, a converted train bridge over Cherry Creek is host to annual Beats on the Creek events put on by the restaurant.

The Beats on the Creek Summer Concert Series benefits Conservation Colorado, which in turn supports clean energy and protects the rivers, outdoor heritage, and public wild lands. The concert series takes over the Wewatta Bridge, one of five remaining railroad crossings that serve as pedestrian bridges over Cherry Creek. The creekside concerts are a vibrant, music-filled party with great local craft cocktails and gourmet appetizers for sale through Coohills.

Chef/owner Tom Coohill opened the highly acclaimed Atlanta restaurant Ciboulette in 1992, which was ranked in the top 10 by *Condé Nast* and in the top 25 nationwide by *Esquire* magazine. Along with his wife, Diane, Tom followed up this success with the also renowned Coohill's: A Steakhouse & Bar in Atlanta. The Rocky Mountains of Colorado called to the outdoor-loving

Many guests stop by Coohills before seeing a concert or game at the nearby Pepsi Center arena.

Top left: Burrata with blackberry jam, fennel cracker, and **Rebel Farms pea** shoots.

Top right: During the summer, windows open to the out**side, letting in warm** breezes and music from Beats on the Creek.

Bottom: *Crème de la glacé*, malted milk ice cream, Laws **sour mash cake,** and whiskey caramel crackers.

couple in 2011, and they established themselves in Denver with the eponymous Coohills Restaurant and Bar.

1400 Wewatta St.
303-623-5700
www.coohills.com
Neighborhood: LoDo

MILE HIGH HAMBURGER MARY'S

Busty blonde comes home to Denver

A staple of the LGBT community, Hamburger Mary's was started in 1972 on a shoestring budget in San Francisco. An open-air bar and grill for open-minded people, the mismatched flatware and kitschy decor became synonymous with made-to-order fresh fare. Locally owned, independent Hamburger Mary's franchises began popping up all over the country, fifteen in all from Hawaii to Illinois.

Of all the Mary's in the country, Mile High Hamburger Mary's is the most intimate, the concept being that the jetsetter Mary comes home to her Mile High abode. In the early 1900s, the present-day Mary's was three Victorian row houses when 17th Avenue had cable tracks and a trolley through the middle of the street, and the two-story homes were those of workers in the area. Joined together in the '40s, the building became a mercantile. In the mid-'70s, the building transformed into a hospitality space, housing Acappella's, known for their cheesesteaks.

Transforming again into a couple of different restaurant varieties, the historic building remained shuttered after the last closing. Previously located further west on 17th St., Mary's came home to roost after an extensive cosmetic renovation, breathing life into the space once again in 2016.

Eat, drink, and be . . . MARY!

Top left: Checks are brought to tables in colorful high heels.

Top right: Juicy burgers, crisp fries, and specialty cocktails are enjoyed at Mile High Hamburger Mary's.

Left: Mary poses under the Colorado flag to welcome guests.

From Drag Queen Bingo to Divas Brunch, to RuPaul and *Will & Grace* watch parties, Mary's is alive with colorful characters. Sourcing local products, Mary's offers a high-end take on a national menu that features favorites such as the **Hula Girl Burger** and **Proud Mary Burger**, and the scratch kitchen uses local, never frozen beef.

1336 E. 17th Ave.
303-993-5812
www.hamburgermarys.com/denver
Neighborhood: Uptown

ROCKY MOUNTAIN CHOCOLATE FACTORY

Small-town chocolate goes international

The quiet town of Durango is located in the southwestern part of the state. Soaring craggy peaks, fresh mountain streams, and the scent of pine permeate the air. Alongside the crisp alpine breeze, wafts of candy and chocolate drift down Main Street from the original Rocky Mountain Chocolate Factory founded by Frank Crail in 1981.

Observing the sleepy mountain town landscape, Crail dreamed of raising his family in this quiet municipality. But this dream hinged on opening a business to support his household, which included seven children. Deciding between a carwash and a candy store, he went with the sweeter option.

Wanting to use marble countertops to prepare the candy, Crail and his business partners found slabs in junkyards, cleaned and shaped them, and created slabs on which the entertaining candy-making process was on display for customers to experience to keep them in the store. Customers can watch the chocolate and caramel being poured, and the open-air kitchen with traditional copper kettles warmed by gas-fired stoves is a staple in the now-franchised company. The in-store candy making demonstrations give insight into the artistry of making caramel apples, fudge, barks, gourmet chocolates, and more.

> "I never imagined that in my search for a place to raise a family things would turn out so sweet!"   —Frank Crail

Left: Beautiful and delicious, the caramel apples are creative, unique, and available in a variety of flavors.

Right: Truffles are especially popular at the Rocky Mountain Chocolate Factory.

Crail took the company public in 1985, and franchises can be found all over the state, country, and globe (including Canada, the Philippines, Japan, the United Arab Emirates, and South Korea). A partnership with Kellogg's in 2014 grew the company further, as it now supplies sweetened corn flakes, almond slices, and chocolate pieces for their family of cereals out of the 53,000-square-foot factory. More than three hundred franchises and $40 million in annual sales have made for a pretty sweet deal for the computer tech turned candyman and his family. The signature oversized Truffles the Bear can be seen at locations, signaling customers that they are in the right spot to enjoy Rocky Mountain Chocolate Factory goodies.

1300 Pearl St.
303-444-8455
www.rmcf.com
Neighborhood: (pictured) Boulder

WORK & CLASS

Approachable cuisine in RiNo

Starting as a dishwasher more than twenty years ago after a family vacation to Colorado, Chef Dana Rodriguez became the protégé of Chef Jennifer Jasinski. Working her way up from dishwater to prep cook to sous chef, Rodriguez's humble beginnings growing up on a farm without running water or electricity in Chihuahua, Mexico, are in sharp contrast to the James Beard–nominated chef she has become today. Taking the leap from hand-grinding corn to making masa for mealtimes, Rodriguez stays true to her authentic and bubbly self. Work & Class is named for the equally approachable restaurant. "It is for working-class people," explains Rodriguez. "You come here to enjoy a square meal, a stiff drink, and a fair price."

Work & Class does not take reservations, and the reclaimed shipping containers that comprise the building—twenty-nine in total, four of them home to the restaurant—are often abuzz with business. Recycled parts can be found throughout the restaurant, from the brake rotors used as chandeliers to the original shipping floors and compressed paper tables. Local whiskeys and beers flow, and four goats are utilized every Monday to provide locally sourced meats for hungry diners. Every pour is two ounces—so out-of-town guests unaccustomed to high elevation should be mindful.

The restaurant closes ten days every year to care for the staff, many of whom have been with Rodriguez from the beginning. Work & Class offers health, dental, 401(k), and paid vacation days, and the

> "Good food, no fuss."   –Chef Dana Rodriguez

Top left: Fresh and flavorful ceviche at Work & Class.

Top right: Lamb and pork meatballs with roasted poblano sauce and queso fresco.

Bottom: Shipping containers are welded together to create the restaurant.

from-the-ground-up restaurant has bloomed into a neighborhood favorite and gathering place.

2500 Larimer St.
303-292-0700
www.workandclassdenver.com
Neighborhood: RiNo

BAROLO GRILL

White truffle paradise

Thanks to an annual staff pilgrimage to Italy, the flavors of Barolo are truly authentic and up to date. The Barolo team celebrates the northern Italian cuisine of the Piedmont region, with its French-inspired flavors and history.

Every November, guests are treated to a white truffle celebration, where the rare delicacy is incorporated into dishes. The restaurant closes around July every year, and the entire staff is flown to the countryside of Italy where they are personally introduced to chefs, winemakers, and other culinary masters. Conversely, winemakers make their way to Colorado for specialty wine-paired dinners and events, completing the cycle of Italy to the Mile High City.

Previously a grocery store and then a jazz club, the space in which Barolo now celebrates its elevated culinary experience began with Blair Taylor and was acquired by Ryan Fletter, who had been the wine director and then general manager. Fletter emphasizes constant growth, education, and innovation.

3030 E. 6th Ave.
303-393-1040
www.barologrilldenver.com
Neighborhood: Cherry Creek

Barolo is home to the most extensive Italian wine list in Denver.

Top left: Locals know to look for this prominent sign on 6th Avenue.

Top right: A comfortable elevated dining room offers guests a superior experience.

Bottom left: Barolo's pasta dishes all but melt in your mouth.

Bottom right: Artfully crafted melon and prosciutto.

URBAN FARMER (page 158)

SARTOS (page 134)

CASA BONITA (page 54)

OLIVE AND FINCH (page 122)

FRASCA (page 72)

VESTA (page 14)

JILL'S RESTAURANT AND BISTRO (page 190)

DOWNTOWN AQUARIUM (page 180)

ACE EAT SERVE (page 136)

ADRIFT TIKI BAR & GRILL (page 28)

BASTIEN'S (page 108)

POSTINO LOHI (page 48)

THE FAMILY JONES (page 58)

BAROLO GRILL (page 82)

HIVE (page 24)

MIETTE ET CHOCOLAT (page 152)

BLUE BONNET (page 154)

LO STELLA

Sail into Portofino

One hundred sixty-five years and counting—Lo Stella Ristorante in Portofino, Italy, is the longest-running family-owned restaurant in the region. Continuing the legacy, eighth-generation Alessandro Polo brings the cuisine of his home country to Denver.

After a twenty-five-year period in Tokyo, Japan, Colorado's mountain beauty called. Polo opened Lo Stella in 2013, welcoming guests to the Golden Triangle neighborhood for a truly authentic Potofino culinary experience. Portofino is one of the most scenic spots on the Mediterranean, and guests can almost taste the essence of the harbor in the authentic cooking of this regional cuisine. Shaped by sailors of the Genoan fleet, the food is historically formulated to celebrate terra firma, with some fish snuck in here and there.

Aromatic herbs, fresh pastas, and garden vegetables combine to make mouthwatering experiences. Fresh basil being a staple of the region, Lo Stella does not shy away from the star ingredient in Denver. The restaurant incorporates Colorado game and fish—a subtle departure from great-grandma's recipes—and the decor evokes Italian flair and memories of ocean air.

1135 Bannock St.
303-825-1995
www.lostelladenver.com
Neighborhood: Lincoln Park

> "Please don't ask me for Alfredo sauce. We're Italian for real!"
> –Alessandro Polo

Top: Photos from the Denver region set the tone for Lo Stella.

Bottom: The dining room is a perfect backdrop for the authentic fare.

ROCKY FORD CANTALOUPE

Summer gems

Encompassing a tri-county area on the Eastern Slope, Rocky Ford is the perfect growing region for melons. Every summer, the region floods the market with delicious vine-ripened melons, which are shipped across the country for sweet, melt-in-your-mouth melon merriment.

This farmland was discovered to be idyllic for melon growth in the late 1800s, and varieties include watermelon and honeydew as well as cantaloupe, with the esteemed title "Rocky Ford grown." Pioneer G. W. Swink originally grew watermelon in the region but later tried his hand at growing the muskmelon for local miners. Native to the Middle East, the muskmelon is a larger cousin of the cantaloupe. The Netted Gem cantaloupes that are a result of that early trial are still extremely popular. Often found prosciutto-wrapped and drizzled in balsamic glaze, or in a gazpacho, or incorporated into a myriad of other restaurant imaginings, the Rocky Ford melons were historically shipped to high-end dining establishments in New York, Chicago, St. Louis, and other locales by passenger train starting in 1895, as an experiment of out-of-state shipping.

Typically taking ninety days from planting to harvest, Rocky Ford cantaloupes start hitting markets in late July, depending on the growing season and weather patterns of the year. The Rocky Ford Growers Association™, founded in 2011, adheres to stringent national safety procedures and places branded stickers on the authentic product, ensuring the sweet and juicy melons are properly identified.

Fresh melons populate menus across the state.

TRY IT

Union Station Farmers Market
1701 Wynkoop St.
303-910-2236
www.bcfm.org/union-station-farmers-market

Mercantile
1701 Wynkoop St., #155
720-460-3733
www.mercantiledenver.com

TAG
1441 Larimer St.
303-996-9985
www.tag-restaurant.com

CONEY ISLAND BOARDWALK

Migrating mega hot dog

In 1966, a group of investors headed by Marcus Shannon hired architect Lloyd Williams to create a very unusual building concept: a 14-ton hot dog. The first of many proposed franchises that Shannon envisioned, the eye-catching Boardwalk at Coney Island was slated for sixteen more diners, which were announced at the grand opening of the original location at 4190 W. Colfax.

Mysteriously shuttered in less than two years, the patented dog concept was listed in a local paper as "hot dog stand for sale," which caught the eye of Beverly Hill, the nation's first female assistant manager of a drive-in theater. Offering $200 as a deposit on the spot, Hill moved the 34-foot hot dog to a parcel of land in Aspen Park, renaming the stand Coney Island Dairyland to avoid patent infringement. The former owners did indeed try to sue but were unsuccessful.

Infuriated locals attempted to have the eye-popping structure removed, as Hill wisely did not announce the placement of the oversized wiener to the community. The proof was in the pudding, however, with more than 1,200 hot dogs sold the first weekend. Hill's stand was open only a year when her husband demanded that she sell. Hill's sister Vervia Goodwin purchased the dog and kept it running for twenty-eight years.

With more than $400,000 in hot dog sales annually, the business was sold for just under $1 million in 1999. The new owners wanted

The first Coney Island hot dog stand was opened in 1871 by Charles Feltman.

A gigantic hot dog welcomes hungry eaters in Bailey.

to develop the property, so the hot dog continued its journey west. Highway 285 had to be closed in both directions as the enormous hot dog traveled to its final resting place on a one-acre lot in Bailey, Colorado. Closed for six years, the re-opened hot dog was a first-date location for John Wallace and Shantelle Stephens, who were scouting locations for a brewery in the 285 corridor and stopped by the attraction on a whim. The couple enjoyed their experience at the unique eatery so much that they eventually bought it and were wed at the location.

The restaurant features local foods, including ketchups, an exclusive-to-Coney mustard, and local produce, and Wallace and Stephens' previous experience in the food and beverage industry serves them well to elevate meals at the Coney Island Boardwalk. Their guests enjoy chili and chocolate sauce made from scratch, grilled hot dogs and sausages, and nostalgia and new beginnings at this favorite haunt.

10 Old Stagecoach Rd.
303-838-9999
Neighborhood: Bailey

BASTIEN'S

Low-key midcentury American dining

In 1937, *Snow White and the Seven Dwarfs* premiered as the first Technicolor, feature-length animated film; Howard Hughes flew from Los Angeles to Newark; Ronald Reagan made his film debut; and the Golden Gate Bridge and the Bastien family's Moon Drive Inn both opened. William Bastien Sr. designed a new building where the Moon Drive Inn stood before it was torn down in 1958. His design for Bastien's was well-received and is listed on the National Register of Historic Places.

Four generations have continued the family tradition, hosting such famed guests as Truman Capote, John Lithgow, Jack Lord, and Chris Daughtry. In addition to families and regular visitors, the nearby Bluebird Theater helps attract local and national acts before or after a show. The nostalgia felt in Bastien's is authentic. The building is carefully preserved, and other restaurants seeking a retro look and feel have tried to emulate its style.

Bastien's famed sugar steak has appeared on *America's Test Kitchen*, but the secret to the multi-ingredient dish was not discovered. The steak was extremely edgy when it was first introduced, but after more than twenty-five years on the menu it continues to bring diners back for more of the satisfying, subtly caramelized crunch.

Many of Bastien's employees have been at the restaurant for more than twenty-five years as well—a true sense of family is felt

"We treat guests how we like to be treated."
–Lara Martin, manager and fourth-generation family member

Above: Tournedos—two 4-ounce filets on toast, topped with hollandaise and asparagus, shown à la Ryan (with jumbo shrimp).

Left: Upstairs dining under a canopy of sparkling lights.

among them. The fundamentals of this historic, trendsetting establishment are a good portion for a good price, and patrons continue to see value in the ever-expanding Denver culinary scene.

3503 E. Colfax Ave.
303-322-0363
www.bastiensrestaurant.com
Neighborhood: South Park Hill

FROZEN MATTER/ RETROGRADE

Cool cache

Couple Gerry Kim and Josh Gertzen have a palate for ice cream. While traveling the world, they found themselves searching for interesting ice cream flavors, savoring sweet experiences, and wondering about the actual craft of ice cream making. The pair come from a legal and tech background, and Kim began baking as a hobby in San Francisco for engagements with friends. Finding the challenge exhilarating and interesting, she began the foray into one of their mutual loves: ice cream.

On a trip to Yosemite, the couple began playing around with the idea of opening their own shop. The name Frozen Matter came up casually, and the idea simmered for about a year. Taking the plunge, they decided to go to ice cream school at a program offered at Penn State. Participating in the 123rd graduating class, the soon-to-be owners of Frozen Matter were told the number one rule of ice cream production for a retailer: buy your base, don't make it yourself.

Not one to shy away from a challenge, Kim and Gertzen decided to create their own base, as they wanted full control of the ingredients of their specialty ice creams. Becoming the only retailer in Colorado to have the license and machinery for their pasteurizer, they now had all aspects of their creamy confections in their hands.

"We wanted to take a culinary approach to ice cream," explains Kim. "Even though it doubles our labor, the approach is the

> "Only crazy people make their own base."
> —Penn State Professor of Ice Cream

110

Left: Creative flavors crafted on-site at Frozen Matter.

Right: Walk through a freezer door at the back of the ice cream shop to enter the Retrograde speakeasy.

direction we wanted to steer our company towards." Formally trained pastry chefs create items to incorporate into the flavors, some of which take two to five days to produce. A unique pairing of beet, honey, and cinnamon creates a flavor known as the Beet Goes On, while house-made cookie dough is incorporated into Chocolate Peanut Butter Cookie Dough and mixed into the carefully prepared custard for flavors.

The high-labor, high-reward ice cream is served alongside ice pops and sodas. Several local retailers have also begun to carry the Denver-made ice cream. Accessible through a faux freezer door in the back of the ice cream shop is Retrograde, a sci-fi retro speakeasy that's a popular Denver destination.

530 E. 19th Ave.
720-600-6358
www.frozenmatter.com
Neighborhood: Uptown

BISTRO VENDÔME

French hideaway in the heart of the city

Off bustling Larimer Square is a hidden French restaurant that transports the diner to a romantic French arrondissement through an open archway that leads to the arcade of the historic Kettle Building at 1420 Larimer Street.

Bistro Vendôme is as warm and comforting as a bowl of French onion soup—one of the timeless classics featured on the menu. A collaboration between chef/owner Jennifer Jasinski, the first Denver chef to win a James Beard Foundation award, and business partner Beth Gruitch. Jasinski honed her culinary skills working for such mentors as Wolfgang Puck at Spago and Jody Denton of Mansion on Turtle Creek fame. General manager/owner Gruitch met Jasinski while they were working together at Panzano.

Besides traditional French fare, Bistro Vendôme offers guests seasonal, farm-fresh dishes. Craveables include poulet roti, quiche du jour, and the classic steak frites with memorable pommes frites with champagne gastrique and herbes de Provence. The café chairs with wooden backs, subway tile floors, and red drapes transport guests to France as steaming dishes come floating from the kitchen.

1420 Larimer St.
303-825-3232
www.bistrovendome.com
Neighborhood: LoDo

Every week Bistro Vendôme goes through sixty pounds of mussels and fifty pounds of flatiron steaks for the three versions of steak frites that are on the menu.

Top left: Petrale sole roulade, zucchini tourné, red peppers, asparagus, pearl onions. beurre blanc, and tobiko caviar.

Top right: Pan-seared Verlasso salmon with hearts of palm, orange segments, grilled avocado, and watercress sauce.

Bottom left: Duck leg confit, morel mushrooms, frisée-herb salad, mustard *crème fraîche*, and red wine gastrique.

Bottom right: Chef Jennifer Jasinski.

POKA LOLA

Deco dish delight

Nestled in the Maven Hotel, Poka Lola Social Club is a mashup of a hipster Art Deco cocktail bar with an Americana turn-of-the-century soda fountain. Poka Lola blends a unique mix of seafoam green leather lounge seating, marble-topped lowboy tables with vintage cocktail sets, and black-and-white Art Deco–style floor tiling. The soda fountain design of the bar was influenced by Red Knapp's Dairy Bar in Rochester, Michigan.

The bar and soda fountain use specialty sourced local ingredients bottled on-site. Poka Lola Social Club is one of Denver's bespoke bar and cocktail lounges in the Dairy Block area. In 1920, H. Brown Canon opened Denver's Windsor Dairy, which was known for its unparalleled quality dairy products. The site of the Windsor Dairy is known today as the Dairy Block, which now houses the Maven Hotel, Poka Lola Social Club, and many other dining and nightlife establishments in Denver's LoDo neighborhood.

From Coney Island hot dogs to hamburger sliders, the nostalgic fare pairs with turn-of-the-century soda and cocktail offerings to accent the look and feel of the space. Whether taking in a game at nearby Coors Field or breaking out a poodle skirt for a sock hop–themed party downtown, Poka Lola is primed for fashionable fare and social gatherings alike.

During World War II, gas shortages forced Windsor Dairy to revert to horse-drawn deliveries. Learning the routes, the horses would habitually stop at the right delivery points.

Above: Barbecue pork sliders pair with craft cocktails at Poka Lola.

Right: Enjoy a game of Foosball while you sip a cocktail or enjoy a light bite.

1850 Wazee St.
720-460-2725
www.pokaloladenver.com
Neighborhood: Ballpark

WINSTON HILL'S RIBS AND STUFF

BBQ with a football history

Winston Hill was an all-star lineman for the New York Jets, playing in the 1969 Super Bowl victory. Hill still holds the Jets record for consecutive games played—a whopping 195. With a knack for longevity that continued with his restaurant, Hill maintained his winning streak when he opened his original barbecue joint off 8th Avenue and Colorado Boulevard in 1977. Originally from Joaquin, Texas, the high school tennis champion turned college football player and All-American was drafted by the Baltimore Colts in 1963 but signed as a free agent with the Jets later that year. Hill retired from football in 1977 and went on to open Winston Hill's Ribs and Stuff in Centennial in 1991.

Bruce Randolf, or "Daddy Bruce," is another football superstar turned entrepreneur. From the '60s to the '90s, he remained a Denver icon, serving food to the homeless every Thanksgiving in front of a local Mercedes dealership. While he was still living, Bruce Randolf Avenue was named in honor of his charitable and community contributions.

Ron Mitchell, Daddy Bruce's second cousin, moved to Denver in 1981 to manage Randolf's restaurant. Hill was mentored by Randolf as well. Mitchell now manages Winston Hill's Ribs and Stuff, marrying iconic recipes and history with slow-cooked meats

"What I learned from Daddy Bruce is simple is better, and shortcuts are bitter."   –Ron Mitchell

Top left: Ron Mitchell prepares the smoker.

Bottom left: Exterior of Winston Hill's Ribs and Stuff.

Right: Ron Mitchell loading the smoker for scrumptious barbecue offerings.

of today. The restaurant still uses hickory wood, and the slow-cooked brisket, turkey, chicken, chorizo, and pork leave visitors with full bellies and smiles on their barbecue-sauce-covered lips.

5090 E. Arapahoe Rd.
303-843-6475
www.winstonhillsribsandstuff.net
Neighborhood: Littleton

117

PANZANO

Northern Italian in Downtown Denver

A historic training ground for some of Denver's best chefs, Panzano has helped many go on to open their own endeavors. The steadfast anchor to the Kimpton Hotel Monaco Denver, this northern Italian eatery churns out Italian fare with flair, offering authentic flavors and bites in a comfortable and inviting space.

The first thing guests often experience at Panzano is the aroma of freshly baked bread. The open-air bakery is a snowstorm of flour. With rows of rising dough and crunchy loaves fresh from the oven, it causes mouths to water even before you're seated. Over the history of the restaurant, the menu has featured a variety of small dishes and over-the-top, belly-bulging entrées. The restaurant is housed in the Hotel Monaco, which opened in 1998 in the joined Railway Exchange Building (built in 1917) and Art Moderne Title Building (built in 1937).

Gleaming copper warms the bar as barrel-aged cocktails are served at this happy hour hot spot. Everything from seasonal pastas and personal pizzas to decadent desserts are received in the dining room overlooking 17th Street. Posh yet still casual, Panzano continues to imbue Italian charm in downtown.

909 17th St.
303-296-3525
www.panzano-denver.com
Neighborhood: Downtown

Creams and butters are typically used in northern Italian cuisine due to the resources of the Alps region.

Top: Salmon atop risotto.

Bottom left: The cheese is not to be missed at Panzano, whether topping a salad, sprinkled over pasta, or enjoyed as a happy hour item.

Bottom right: The dining room looks out to the bustling city beyond.

BIJU'S LITTLE CURRY SHOP

Bold Colorado Curry

Fueled by a healthy lifestyle, Chef Biju Thomas transferred his love of being a competitive cyclist to a passion for being a culinarian. Originally from Kerala, India, Thomas's vibrant and healthy lifestyle continues in the Mile High City.

Thomas partnered with Dr. Allen Lim to create the *Feed Zone* cookbook series in 2009, and he began cooking for athletes and celebrities.

Thomas launched a new entrepreneurial endeavor in 2014 with the opening of the first Biju's Little Curry Shop in RiNo, or the River North neighborhood. The fast-casual dishes don't skimp on flavor, as the aromas wafting through the air can attest. Vibrant curries, house-made chili lime salt, and chilled Kombucha make for a perfect lunch bite, as guests build bowls, adding spice and condiments to their liking. The lighter preparations of coconut curries, vindaloo, and chutneys are a welcome addition to the culinary scene, as Thomas continues to win accolades in Denver and beyond.

1441 26th St.
303-292-3500
www.littlecurryshop.com
Neighborhood: RiNo

Top: Curries, rice, and meats ready for hungry customers at Biju's Little Curry Shop.

Bottom: Coconut curry chicken bowl: biriyani with spiced lentils, coconut curry chicken with sauteed cabbage, herb yogurt, and a splash of cilantro and mint chutney with crushed papadam.

OLIVE AND FINCH

Foodie fast-casual

Finches are known for working morning to night, waking up early to go about their birdy business. Olives are translatable into many various types of cuisine, from sweet to savory, simple to complex. The same can be said about chef/owner Mary Nguyen, an early riser who enjoys her work and translates her ingredients into a wide variety of delicious creations.

When she opened Olive and Finch in 2013, Nguyen had been looking for a restaurant where she wanted to eat but that wouldn't require a huge time commitment or cause her to spend an arm and a leg for a well-rounded, quality meal. Not being able to find such a venue in the Denver market at the time, she decided to open her own.

Olive and Finch bakes its own bread, roasts and hand carves its own chickens and turkeys, and hand makes pastries daily. Serving quality food on a quick timeline, Nguyen's eatery offers a full-service dining experience boiled down to a counter-style delivery, and Denverites love it. To meet the demand for Nguyen's concept, a second location opened in Cherry Creek. Expanding had not been part of the original plan for Olive and Finch, but as Mary rightfully acknowledged, the demand for her restaurant was the tipping point for another location.

1552 E. 17th Ave.
303-832-8663
www.oliveandfincheatery.com
Neighborhood: Uptown

Finches are very social birds and prefer to be in pairs or flocks.

Above: Bogota hash with coffee, fresh fruit, and a house-made beignet.

Right: An assortment of from-scratch pastries: vanilla confetti cake, gluten-free coconut cake, raspberry mousse cake, Grandma's carrot cake, and a fresh fruit tart.

TRUFFLE TABLE

Elevating cheese in LoHi

Serviced by the Truffle Cheese Shop in Cherry Creek, Truffle Table is Denver's oldest cheese restaurant in the city. The shop, which opened in 2013, may offer cheeses that have been aging longer than the shop has been in business, but the specialized eatery is a must-stop while exploring the Lower Highlands neighborhood.

Cut-to-order cheeses are crafted by artisan producers at the Truffle Table. If the shop cannot reach the producer by phone and have a direct connection, they do not carry the cheese. A tight-knit and carefully curated collection of cheeses is accompanied by shareable plates and a cheese-friendly wine program.

Couple Karin and Robert Lawler opened the mom-and-pop shop to educate the community about cheese. It's the oldest produced food in human history not grown from the ground, and it's easy to get lost in the complex world of cheese. In lieu of servers, each staff member is a working cheesemonger. Picking the cheeses for the plates, enlightening apprehensive guests, and pairing with exquisite wines, Truffle Table is an effortless extension of the cheese shop's offerings.

All-you-can-eat raclette offerings make the no-reservations spot a hotbed of ooey gooey goodness every Wednesday. Other specials are sprinkled throughout the week, and the space is open five days a

> The size of the curd results in the softness of the cheese, with large curds making for soft cheeses and small curds for harder varieties.

Left: Marinated olives burst with flavor and citrus tones.

Right: Crafted to perfection, the Monger's Choice cheese and cured meat board will leave you breathless.

week with happy hour every day. The unique five-point intersection outside the 1890s building makes for a long, pointed space and provides dinner drama for diners enjoying the outdoor patio.

2556 15th St.
303-455-9463
www.truffletable.com
Neighborhood: LoHi

PENROSE ROOM

Five-star, five-diamond dining

During the 1950s and 1960s, an increase in tourism allowed for expansion at the legendary Broadmoor Resort. Opened in 1961, the South Tower would become home to the newest culinary addition to the property: the Penrose Room, named for the high-spirited founder of the Broadmoor, Spencer Penrose, and his wife, Julie Penrose.

A fine-dining experience at an already luxurious hotel, the ninth-floor Penrose Room boasts European-inspired cuisine to continue the tradition today. During an extensive renovation of the South Tower in 2006, floor-to-ceiling windows were installed in the Penrose Room, which provide sweeping views of the mountains and lake below. A chef's kitchen and balcony were also added.

Under the guidance of Executive Chef Louis Stratta, the Broadmoor soared into virgin territory for Colorado, offering elevated dining experiences only found in other parts of the world until then. Now under the guidance of accomplished Executive Chef David Patterson, the sixth executive chef in the history of the world-famous resort, the gourmet offerings continue to excel.

1 Lake Ave.
719-577-5773
www.broadmoor.com/dining/penrose-room
Neighborhood: Colorado Springs

Spencer Penrose financed several projects in Colorado Springs, including the Broadmoor, the Cheyenne Mountain Zoo, the Will Rogers Shrine of the Sun, and the Pikes Peak Highway. He also established the El Pomar Foundation.

Top left: A beautiful beef tartare from the Penrose Room.

Bottom left: Honey-lacquered Rohan duck breast.

Right: Herb-roasted Green Circle Farm chicken breast.

BOULDER DUSHANBE TEAHOUSE

Tea-jikistan tie-in

Sister city to Dushanbe, Tajikistan, in Central Asia, Boulder began its siblingship in 1987, when artists from Tajikistan visited Boulder to design a unique building for the city. In 1990, forty artisans completed construction in their far-off country, then disassembled the building and shipped its pieces to Boulder in more than two hundred crates.

Beautifully intricate hand-painted, hand-carved, and hand-hewn elements of the impressive building sat in limbo for eight years while the city decided who should run such an enterprise. Lenny and Sara Martinelli met while working in the service industry and bid on the project to open as a traditional teahouse. Lenny's almost forty years in the culinary business paired with his interest in architecture made for a perfect outlet for him and Sara to express their creativity.

Winning the bid and grant to construct the teahouse, the Martinellis were able to bring artisans from Tajikistan to assemble the teahouse—a process that took nine months. Filling the new location with more than a hundred teas and global cuisine, the traditional place for gathering in Asian culture has become a popular gathering place in the Boulder foothills.

"Dushanbe" means Monday in the Tajik language. The city's name comes from a popular market that was originally held there on Mondays.

Top left: Blooming teas come in several flavors.

Top right: Intricate carvings and artwork decorate the interior of the Boulder Dushanbe Teahouse.

Bottom left: Colorful dishes and food from a diverse global background converge at the teahouse.

Bottom right: Personal tea service.

1770 13th St.
303-442-4993
www.boulderteahouse.com
Neighborhood: Boulder

ENSTROM'S

Unpretentious success on the Western Slope

Chet Enstrom started a candy empire as a hobby, humbly amazed at how many people continued to order his product. Enstrom's goal in life was to do his best, give his all, and help his community, which were all accomplished and led to a multigenerational family-owned business that still leads the way in candy in Colorado today.

Moving from Colorado Springs to Grand Junction, Enstrom and business partner Harry Jones opened the Jones-Enstrom Ice Cream Company in March 1929. The Great Depression began in October of that year, yet the company persevered, weathering the storm without laying off any employees and not missing a single payday.

In 1934, Enstrom dusted off his candy-making skills, which he had developed in Colorado Springs. Initially using the family kitchen in his home, he eventually moved to the basement, where he set up a primitive candy-making operation. Far from the commercial enterprise it was to become, Enstrom didn't even charge for the candy he created during the colder winter months when ice cream sales were slow. He gave away the hand-dipped caramels and toffees to the dairymen who he bought cream from for the ice cream for the holidays. He also gave candy to his children's teachers.

During World War II, rationed sugar was magically transformed into sweet treats for the troops. Family members of servicemen brought sugar bowls to Enstrom who furnished the rest of the ingredients at no charge. The charitably minded Enstrom continued

Enstrom's world-famous toffee was served at the captain's table on the final voyage of the RMS *Queen Elizabeth*.

Left: Chet Enstrom. Photo courtesy of Enstrom.
Right: Production at the Grand Junction plant.

to bring smiles to those around him and abroad with homemade delights.

Monthly flavors were a staple of Jones-Enstrom ice cream. But on one occasion, Enstrom didn't have a flavor profile idea as a new month approached, so he started to experiment with a candy concept he came up with after getting a piece of toffee from a traveling salesman. He created his own concoction to chop up and put in vanilla ice cream, and the new flavor was dubbed Butter Brickle.

By 1954, the popular candy side of the business was bursting at the seams and needed its own space. More than four thousand pounds of almond toffee was being produced by 1959, so the following year Enstrom sold the ice cream business to focus on candy. He and his wife, Vernie, planned to make candy during the winter and golf during the summer. The popular candy grew the business into a full-time operation, and after being appointed to the state senate, Chet bequeathed the company to his son Emil.

Today, more than seven thousand pounds of chocolate rest in tanks waiting for production, and six kettles boil with expectant toffee. Copper kettles are used as the conductor, and a 1929 turtle machine still creates edible adorable critters. Hand-done enrobing of chocolate and hand-checked product makes for a labor-intensive process, which is under the watchful eye of brothers Doug Jr. and Jim Simons, great-grandsons of Chet. The 1,000 lbs/hour natural butter toffee cooker is the only one in the world and a closely kept secret of engineering. Little waste goes into production, as the chocolate, toffee, and nut dust and crumbs from manufacturing are used in other products, such as cookies and baking supplies.

More than ninety-six thousand gallons of chocolate are delivered by tanker to the production facility in Grand Junction, which makes witnessing the Enstrom's assembly rooms a Willy Wonka–esque experience. Hand-broken slabs of toffee can be seen through a viewing window as employees with an average of eight to twelve years of experience expertly craft the Colorado chocolate. A Denver retailer of the Colorado confections can be found in Cherry Creek.

201 University Blvd., #118
303-322-1005
www.enstrom.com
Neighborhood: Cherry Creek

Enstrom's Cherry Creek retail location is a candy lover's dream.

SARTO'S

Tailor-made fare

Verona, Italy—the stage for *Romeo and Juliet*, one of history's great romances—also set the stage for one of Denver's most beautiful dining experiences. Opened in 2014 in a building that was originally a fabric shop in the '50s, Sarto's ("tailor" in Italian) has several elegant and thoughtful touches throughout—pinstripe fabric reminiscent of men's suits, a three-fold mirror near the restrooms, and gleaming Carrara marble countertops in the bright, white space.

While visiting the famed northern Italian city of Verona, owner Taylor Swallow and his wife had lunch across from a tailor's shop whose sign read, "Sarto." Not wanting to name the restaurant after himself, Swallow leaned in to the tailored concept of Sarto's. The restaurant is home to Denver's only *cicchetti* bar, or *bacari*, and small plates pepper the menu as well as Aperol-inspired cocktail concoctions. Interactive in nature, the bar is a gathering place to visit with friends and enjoy the authentic fare. The full-scratch kitchen neighbors the bakery and pastry chef station, and the Pantry adjacent to Sarto's offers grab-and-go handmade pastas and take-and-bake opportunities to take home a piece of the tailored experience.

2900 W. 25th Ave.
303-455-1400
www.sartos.com
Neighborhood: Jefferson Park

Tracing its beginnings back to the twelfth century, tailoring (or "to cut") began to modify clothing to accentuate rather than conceal the body.

Above: Unique dishes, such as this black-squid-ink pasta, offer an uncommon take on Italian food.

Left: Caprese with watermelon radishes and balsamic reduction.

ACE EAT SERVE

Ping-pong play

Stepping into Ace Eat Serve is akin to visiting a foreign country: the Asian regional cuisine aromas waft into the air, cold specialty beers and unique sakes are served in chilly glasses and cans, and the sounds of ping-pong and laughter echo throughout the restaurant.

Previously the Storz Garage, a limousine warehouse in the Uptown neighborhood, Ace now is home to eight ping-pong tables inside and four concrete tables outside for a unique dining experience fostered by Asian inspiration. Classic takes on traditional dishes pair with the atmosphere, with house-made bao buns made daily and stuffed with flavorful fillings alongside spicy tiger wings paired with chilly Tiger beer imported from Asia.

Old reclaimed shipping containers and bamboo bar tops transport guests to far-off lands while an antique shaved ice maker from Thailand churns icy treats to cool down the afternoon. More than eighty whiskeys and a variety of Asian beers create a plethora of pairings, and a vintage VW bar bus pops open on the patio or for off-premise events.

With the restaurant's decor and design complementing the history of the building, Ace received the 2012 Mayor's Design Award for Denver. So whether grabbing a paddle to pummel playful

> The restaurant's made-from-scratch fortune cookies feature unique tongue-in-cheek fortunes that include '80s and '90s song lyrics such as "I'd do anything for love, but I won't do that."

Top left: Ping-pong tables are the focal point of this unique destination.

Bottom left: Ramen is available in several flavors.

Right: Whether enjoying a Shanghai pork belly bun (pictured), a Korean fried chicken bun, or a miso eggplant bun, the bao buns are not to be missed.

ping-pong balls across the table or sliding a chilly foreign beer down the bar, this unique eatery is worth savoring all the experiences to be had.

501 E. 17th Ave.
303-800-7705
www.aceeatserve.com
Neighborhood: Uptown

ROCKY MOUNTAIN OYSTERS

Western delicacy

It's hard not to get squeamish thinking about the source of Rocky Mountain oysters (cattle testicles), but the long-running history of the Western delicacy is undeniable.

Organ meats have a running history in the West, from Native Americans utilizing every aspect of hunted animals to ranchers preparing the protein-rich grub in the plains and mountains alike. Other cheeky nicknames, such as "cowboy caviar," "dusted nuts," and "Montana tendergroins," may leave some diners rolling their eyes instead of ordering the dish, but the deep-fried plates continue to fly off the kitchen lines in Denver.

Usually served with dipping sauces, the meat is typically served peeled, pounded flat, sliced, coated in flour, and then fried. Nicknamed oysters because of their slimy appearance when raw, prairie oysters can also be made from pigs, lambs, beef, and bison.

TRY IT

Buckhorn Exchange–Available as a whole or half order, served with horseradish sauce.
1000 Osage St.
303-534-9505
www.buckhornexchange.com

Rocky Mountain oysters from the Buckhorn Exchange.

Coors Field–A Rocky Mountain Po'Boy is available through
Aramark, the stadium's concessions provider.
2001 Blake St.
www.mlb.com/rockies/ballpark

The Fort–"The last thing to jump over the fence" is served
with tangy sweet chili sauce.
19192 Colorado Hwy. 8
303-697-4771
www.thefort.com

MIZUNA

Doyenne of Denver dining

The exterior of Mizuna is charming yet unassuming, but inside beats a lionheart of a restaurant. Mizuna has offered Denver diners a polished and sumptuous culinary experience since chef/owner Frank Bonanno and late partner Doug Fleischmann opened the doors in 2001. The staff provide warm and attentive service, from the host to the sommelier, but make no mistake, this is a chef's restaurant through and through. The quality of the ingredients drives the menu, where dishes are the result of a nod to tradition, creativity is highly encouraged but not at the expense of taste, and each plate is a thing of unapproachable beauty. It's all about the food.

The interior is classic and inviting. The open kitchen allows a glimpse into a well-choreographed dance among the white-jacketed chefs. Mizuna is an ideal restaurant for milestone celebratory dinners or for enjoying a bowl of their famed butter poached Maine lobster macaroni & cheese, on the menu since opening, with a glass of perfectly paired dry Riesling at the small bar if you are lucky enough to find an open barstool.

Bonanno can still be found on the line at Mizuna some nights, which is remarkable considering he is dedicated to his family, hosts the show *Chef Driven* on PBS, and heads Bonanno Concepts, a restaurant family that includes ten unique, stand-alone restaurants. Bonanno's most recent project was opening sixteen, yes, that is right, *sixteen* restaurants on the same day in Denver's newest food hall/multioutlet eatery, Denver Milk Market.

> The row of restaurants that Bonanno Concepts owns adjacent to Mizuna has been dubbed part of the "Bonanno block."

Left: Beef Wellington with broccoli custard, potatoes Anna, and veal demi-glace.
Right: Warm chocolate cake with malted vanilla ice cream and macadamia brittle.

If that is not enough to illustrate the important role Bonanno has played in developing the food culture of Denver, consider that Mizuna has also served as the training ground and launch pad for fourteen chefs who graduated to open their own successful restaurants . . . and Frank is just as passionate about food today as ever.

225 E. 7th Ave.
303-832-4778
www.mizunadenver.com
Neighborhood: Speer

GREEN CHILI

Colorado comfort food

While not green in color at all, the secret ingredient to the saucy consistency is the green chili. Typically prepared with pork, the chili is used on Denver omelets, smothered on hamburger patties called "sloppers," and incorporated into spicy grilled cheese sandwiches. It can also be enjoyed on its own in a bowl or with chips to dip.

Green chilis can be found prepared all over the state, from roadside stands to restaurants, grocery stores, and mercantiles. Hatch green chilis are grown in Hatch, New Mexico, while Pueblo green chilis are grown five hundred miles north in Pueblo, Colorado. In a friendly rivalry with neighboring New Mexico, the debate can sometimes get as spicy as the ingredients.

TRY IT

Morning Collective
2160 S. Broadway
303-953-9943
www.morningcollective.com

GRIND kitchen + watering hole
300 Fillmore St.
720-749-4158
www.grinddenver.com

Patzcuaro's Mexican Restaurant
2616 W. 32nd Ave.
303-455-4389
www.patzcuaros.com

Whether as a side, an entree, or a sauce, green chili is popular throughout Colorado.

D BAR

d-licious Denver dining

Drinks. Dining. Dessert. D Bar in Uptown has been thrilling diners since opening at its original location on 17th Avenue in 2008 and moving to their new location in 2015 with chef/owners Keegan Gerhard and Lisa Bailey. Gerhard, a Food Network celebrity chef, and Bailey, one of the top pastry chefs in America, team up to make unforgettable dining experiences.

Drawn to Colorado after traveling consistently with *Food Network Challenge* and shooting thirty episodes a year on the road, Gerhard began shooting more episodes locally with High Noon Productions, which coincidentally is also based in Colorado. Bailey had worked on her thesis in Texas on opening a B&B inspired by Colorado. Agreeing that Denver diners wanted to have choices when going out and that a restaurant didn't need to be everything to everyone, the couple envisioned D Bar. The original concept was a dessert bar where guests could come after their meals to enjoy a sweet treat, but two weeks before opening their doors, the duo decided to add savory, non-dessert options to the menu.

"Things We Like to Eat" still remains a section on today's menu, creating both a dinner rush and a dessert rush at the popular restaurant. Ninety percent of guests order dessert per table, which is staggering in an industry where dessert can be a hard sell to guests. The restaurant is famous for its "cake and shake" (a mini vanilla, chocolate, or raspberry milkshake and petite slice of three-layer chocolate cake with Madagascar chocolate frosting), and Chef

> "We aim to be better than yesterday, not as good as tomorrow."
> —Chef Keegan Gerhard

Left: Colorado lamb gyro with lemon garlic fries.

Top right: Chef/owners Lisa Bailey and Keegan Gerhard.

Bottom right: The enticing desserts at D Bar are delicious and beautiful.

Keegan was the first person to appear on the cover of the popular *Westword* newspaper and the first chef welcome voiceover on the train from Denver International Airport. Inspired by cuisine and unique experiences, D Bar is a focused culinary sanctuary that's a beacon to those with both a sweet tooth and a savory palate. The restaurant creates menu items with a twist that guests know well.

494 E. 19th Ave.
303-861-4710
www.dbardenver.com
Neighborhood: Uptown

RANGE

Where the deer and the antelope . . . never mind

Grilling, smoking, roasting, cast-iron sautéing, pickling, and preserving—all are techniques found at range, a restaurant celebrating cultural heritage and adventurous spirit within the former Colorado National Bank building.

Listed on the National Register of Historic Places, the Colorado National Bank building was designed by famed Denver architects William and Arthur Fisher. It was originally erected as a four-story building in 1915 on the corner of 17th & Champa Streets in downtown Denver, an area dubbed the Wall Street of the Rockies. The building's neoclassic, Greek Revival architecture is highlighted in its towering white exterior columns and walls, created with marble from the Colorado Yule Marble Company—the same marble that was being used the year it was built to erect the Lincoln Memorial in Washington, D.C. Large monogrammed bronze doors opened to the three-story interior atrium featuring marble flooring, ornate bronze accents, and the most secure vaults in existence at the time, with doors weighing sixty thousand pounds.

After a meticulous restoration, the building's lobby features sixteen original oil-on-canvas murals by renowned Western artist Allen Tupper True. Titled *Indian Memories*, these murals are among True's most famous. Some of his other prominent works include murals in the Wyoming, Missouri, and Colorado state capitols, as well as Wyoming's bucking horse symbol featured on the state's

Downstairs from range, the former bank vaults have been converted to meeting rooms and event spaces.

Above: range's menu offers a multitude of butcher's cuts, each served with a gourmet side dish and house-made sauces.

Right: It's not all about meat at range; locally sourced vegetable dishes also shine.

license plate. The murals consist of five triptychs, each named after and demonstrating a different aspect of Native American life, including "Youth," "Buffalo Hunt," "War," "Women," and "Art Work." The series concludes with "Happy Hunting Ground," a much larger mural.

918 17th St.
720-726-4800
www.rangedowntown.com
Neighborhood: Downtown

THE TABLETOP TAP

A gamer's oasis

A 1980s arcade machine might seem like a strange choice for a housewarming gift, but that's exactly what Jason Ungate got for his wife Kristin when they moved into their sparse home. Although still a favorite game of theirs, Joust is no longer the only arcade in their home. After filling their house with seventeen other arcade cabinets, Jason was told he wasn't allowed to bring any more to the house. Problem solved: build a bar.

The Tabletop Tap opened in 2018 with more than 120 board games, 100 arcade games built into the bar, and 5 stand-up cabinets. Serving twenty beers on tap, the constantly rotating options feature three or four IPAs and old favorites that cycle through. A favorite of the Ungates is a Campfire Stout from High Water Brewing that tastes like s'mores in a glass.

Pairing their brew offerings with local Hospo's Pizza is a perfect way to finish off a game of Mario Kart or Harry Potter trivia.

Previously home to other retailers, the building has been everything from a vape shop to a Catholic ecumenical supply store. With his work cut out for him, Ungate aimed to create a truly

Arcade games from the '80s and '90s, such as Mortal Kombat, Golden Axe, Gauntlet, and Pac-Man, can be found within the custom bar at Tabletop Tap.

Left: Hospo's Pizza is available in cheese, pepperoni, sausage/pepperoni, supreme, meat (bacon, Canadian bacon, pepperoni, and sausage), barbecue chicken, buffalo chicken, and white.

Right: Sip a beer at the the Tabletop Tap and play a plethora of games on innovative systems built into the bar surface.

unique experience for his patrons. By offering gaming within the bar itself, with controllers accessed below the bar top for play, he believes he's created a first-of-its-kind gaming experience.

Whether participating in a Dungeons & Dragons tournament or leveling up on Galaga, you or your team can make the Tabletop Tap your abode for an afternoon or evening of gaming fun.

3394 S. Broadway
720-287-0155
www.tabletoptap.com
Neighborhood: Englewood

SOUTH PEARL STREET FARMERS MARKET

Rural roots

Shoppers can be found browsing the selections at the farmers market on historic South Pearl Street for a whopping twenty-seven weeks of the year. Started as a single-day event in 2001 with just ten vendors, the market has grown to become one of the go-to's in Denver, with now more than a hundred vendors. From fresh Western Slope produce to mushrooms, from microgreens to jellies and jams, the extent of the market is incredible.

Brown Dog Farm of Golden, Colorado, is one vendor that brings bountiful products to the market. Named for their brown dog Waco that has been with owners Tim and Bessie since beginning their journey in Texas, Brown Dog Farm opened in the foothills of Golden in 2013. The farm specializes in greens, radishes, and turnips, and the Easter egg radishes glisten from a fresh spritz of water as visitors admire their colorful harvest.

Started in 1907, Ela Family Farms is just down the row from Brown Dog. At the farm, Steve Ela, the fourth generation of fruit tree farmers, helps customers pick the perfect peach for which the farm is known. More than sixty varieties of fruit are grown on the farm, which contains one hundred acres of certified organic orchards. Take a bite of a peach, and the juice will run down your chin.

> More than a hundred farmers markets can be found throughout Colorado, happening on different days of the week and with different specialties.

Left: Easter egg radishes from Brown Dog Farm.

Center: Steve Ela shows off peaches from Ela Family Farms.

Right: Mushrooms offered by Mile High Fungi.

A newcomer to the bazaar, Mile High Fungi has been offering their several varieties of mushrooms at the market since 2017. Owners Michael and Liz Nail, who run a true mom-and-pop shop, rely on farmers markets and community involvement to continue bringing their sustainable mushrooms to patrons. Starting with the Cottage Food Act for small production, the couple dipped their toe into what is now a thriving mushroom business full of varietals, such as shiitake, lion's mane, and king trumpet.

www.southpearlstreet.com/farmers-market
Neighborhood: Washington Park

MIETTE ET CHOCOLAT

Crumbs and Chocolate

David Lewis and Gonzalo Jimenez have come together to create quite a duo in the refurbished Stanley Marketplace, previously an aircraft hangar. At Miette et Chocolat, which translates to "crumbs and chocolate," the sweet treats beckon from gleaming cases. Delightful creations include Snickers tarts, Nutella eclairs, and crunchy hazelnut mousse bars.

Opened in 2016, the collaboration between chefs began before they opened the doors of Miette. The small but well-rounded operation incorporates each of the chefs' skill sets—chocolates and pastries—to create a unique, more expansive setup. Originally from rural Illinois, Lewis served previously as executive pastry chef at the Brown Palace. He met Jimenez at a 2009 competition in Atlanta, where they created chocolate sculptures as part of a team. Jimenez was born in Argentina, and his chocolatier culinary career has taken him all over the Americas, including St. Julien in Boulder, Colorado. While Jimenez was in Santiago, Chile, and Lewis was in Denver, the two hatched the plan for Miette et Chocolat via FaceTime.

Production happens at a nearby facility, but the window into the pastry shop for baked goods at Stanley Marketplace is a wonderland of ingredients and culinary acumen on display. One of the few places in Colorado to make its chocolate from scratch, Miette's bean-to-bar approach puts its own product on display in its own retail storefront. Its ingredients are also in local beer development and in chocolate sauce for nearby donut retailers, and other candy stores sell its bars of Colorado-crafted chocolate.

The alien-esque cacao pods are on display but not for sale. Guests are invited to look but not touch.

Left: Retail offerings at Miette et Chocolat.
Right: Fruit tarts almost too beautiful to eat.

A Wyoming snow fence was utilized as the backdrop to the shop, and the silvery greys are a perfect accent to the rich and warm chocolate hues ranging from small truffles to large sculptures on display. Cacao pods pepper the store, so guests can see the very beginnings of the arduous process of chocolate making. Whisks from old beaters create the lighting elements for a cozy yet detail-oriented space in the former cavernous hangar.

2501 Dallas St., Ste. 176
303-658-0861
www.mietteetchocolat.com
Neighborhood: Stapleton

BLUE BONNET

Nacho mamma's enchiladas

Mexican restaurants flood the Denver culinary scene—taco bars, burrito stands, and guacamole consumed at a rapid pace. One distinctive restaurant that has withstood the trials of time is Blue Bonnet, purchased by Philip and Arlene Mobell in 1968.

After Philip and Arlene's retirement, siblings Gary and Marci took over the restaurant, named after the Texas bluebonnet flower. Moving the restaurant to its current location on bustling Broadway in 1994, the Mexican mainstay continues serving longtime patrons and tourists alike.

Flights of mini margaritas pair with the restaurant's famous chimichanga, chips and salsa, and chili rellenos. Longtime employee Luis Galvez began his career at Blue Bonnet as a dishwasher in 1994. Now head chef, he incorporates new menu items to accentuate old standbys, and many of his additions are inspired by his mother's recipes from Mexico.

457 S. Broadway
303-778-0147
www.bluebonnetrestaurant.com
Neighborhood: Baker

Blue Bonnet goes through twenty thousand pounds of tortillas, one thousand pounds of cheese, and eight hundred gallons of salsa a week.

Top: Traditional dishes and new takes on Mexican food are found throughout the menu.

Bottom left: A flight of mini-margaritas.

Bottom right: Ceviche with avocado and lime.

CUBA CUBA

Flavors of the Caribbean

Kristy Socarras Bigelow fled Cuba in 1959 at the age of twelve, and her mother had imbued Cuban culture in her since birth. Creating her own slice of Cuban paradise in Denver, Socarras Bigelow opened the doors of Cuba Cuba in 2001.

Infused with Cuban culture by four generations of Cuban relatives in Miami, Socarras Bigelow grew up with the zest of the island with massive spreads of Cuban food, Latin music, and festive parties. Not allowed to go to college by her mother, she moved to Denver to pursue a career in social work. Craving familiar tastes and culture, she was unable to locate favorite dishes in the Mile High City.

Located in two combined Victorian-era houses, Cuba Cuba opened complete with a metal palm tree outside. The memorable aromas of Cuban cuisine trail through the air as blithely as the expressive Latin music. Mojitos, *vaca frita*, and fried plantains join a plethora of menu items previously absent in the city. At Cuba Cuba, Socarras Bigelow has created the utopian paradise that she dreamed of while hearing tales from her family in Miami. The energy ignited by her is contagious, fostering community in the Golden Triangle.

1173 Delaware St.
303-605-2822
www.cubacubacafe.com
Neighborhood: Lincoln Park

"*Mi Cuba es su Cuba!*"   –Kristy Socarras Bigelow

Top left: Exterior of Cuba Cuba.

Top right: With food as colorful as the interior, the entire establishment is alive with vibrant hues.

Bottom left: Tres leches cake topped with merengue.

Bottom right: Pollo a la Plancha: butterflied chicken breast, mojo marinade, white rice, black beans, and tostones.

URBAN FARMER

Cattle drive on Wazee

The Oxford Hotel is Denver's oldest hotel. It opened in 1891 a short walk from Union Station, the lifeblood of the city for train travel at the time. The hotel boasts a rich history of colorful characters, a power plant of its own, whispered speakeasys during Prohibition, and in-hotel stables. Today Urban Farmer joins the quilt of history at the Oxford Hotel, adding its own unique attributes.

The mushroom terrarium in the basement is one of several unique aspects of Urban Farmer. The steakhouse's seasonally driven menu curated by Executive Chef Chris Starkus incorporates a nose-to-tail, whole animal butchery program; a local cheese assortment; and indigenous honeys to boot.

A neon sign can be seen from the street, utilizing David Bowie's words: "I don't know where I'm going from here, but I promise it won't be boring." The transparent food approach is anything but boring, as lively combinations of cuisine artfully adorn dishes coming from the kitchen.

1659 Wazee St.
303-262-6070
www.urbanfarmerdenver.com
Neighborhood: LoDo

Every January, forty longhorn cattle are driven up 17th Street for the Denver Stock Show cattle drive right in front of Urban Farmer.

Top: Ice block shrimp cocktail with spicy tomato jam, pickled red onion, and cucumber.

Bottom left: Neon sign art in the dining room.

Bottom right: Foie gras served at Urban Farmer.

JUST BE KITCHEN

Healthy comfort food

Jennifer Peters transitioned into the restaurant business after leaving a corporate job, with the aim to provide guests a place to feel fulfilled, safe, and nourished. She started Just BE Kitchen in 2017, and the modification-friendly restaurant provides a menu that satisfies a wide array of dietary restrictions and eating preferences.

Located in Denver near Confluence Park and the Platte River, Just BE Kitchen is open for breakfast, lunch, and dinner. The cheerful dining room serves farm-fresh food fast, with the goal to nourish the body with appropriate foods to allow diners to reach their highest potential. Positive messages adorn the walls, and helpful staff guide guests through the menu with dietary restrictions and goals in mind. Whether you're looking for gluten free, dairy free, vegan, or sugar free, the waitstaff and kitchen team will cook something up that's not only to your specific needs but also doesn't sacrifice on flavor.

As she persistently pursued her goal of opening Just BE Kitchen, Peters was turned down repeatedly for not having a history in the restaurant industry. Staying true to her mission to help change the world, through trials and disappointments, Peters's perseverance continues to inspire, as she shares her truth and positive attitude through her venture.

2364 15th St.
303-284-6652
www.justbekitchen.com
Neighborhood: Jefferson Park

"Integrity. It's a must, and it's sexy."   —Jennifer Peters

Above: Inspiring artwork adorns the walls at Just BE Kitchen.

Left: The Fulfilled breakfast burrito with scrambled eggs, sausage, "cheddar wiz," paleo tortilla, sweet potato hash, pork or veggie green chili, cilantro, scallion, and jalapeño.

PALISADE PEACHES

Georgia's jealousy

I s it possible for candy to grow on trees? In Palisade, Colorado, yes. Peach season is something most Coloradans look forward to. The more than $21 million industry annually produces more than ten thousand tons of the sweet treats.

In 1882, John and Jean Harlow planted some of the first trees, testing the soil of Palisade in the Grand Valley. With warm winds coming off the surrounding mesas and water from the Colorado River, the area is perfect for peaches. In the early 1900s, twenty-five thousand pounds of peaches were produced and shipped daily around the region. Today the peaches appear on menus around the state and are shipped all over the country. According to the U.S. Department of Agriculture, more than ten thousand tons were grown in 2017.

Running down the chins of eager eaters, peach juice from tree-ripened peaches is a special annual treat. Bushels of the fruit are sold in farmers markets, grocery stores, and roadside fruit stands, with the taste of mountain sunshine emanating from the vibrant summer fruit.

TRY IT

Colorado Fresh Markets
303-442-1837
www.coloradofreshmarkets.com

Bastien's Peach Sizzling Skillet Pie (seasonal dessert special)
3503 E. Colfax Ave.
303-322-0363
www.bastiensrestaurant.com

Sweet treats: Palisade peaches are a Colorado favorite.

Frozen Matter peaches & cream ice cream
530 E. 19th Ave.
720-600-6358
www.frozenmatter.com

RISTORANTE DEL LAGO

Lakeside dining

The lake at the Broadmoor has been home to many a spectacle, from historic water skiing to resident sea lions of days past, to contemporary Lightning Bug wooden boats and majestic swans. Overlooking the centerpiece of the property is Ristorante and Bar del Lago.

Charles Court, the footprint of what is now del Lago, opened in 1976 as part of the Broadmoor West expansion. Traditional European cuisine graced the menu of Charles Court under the guidance of Master Chef Herbert J. Uerdingen, who had been with the property since 1962. Hand-blown glass chandeliers and napkin rings added to the dining ambience of Charles Court, with the blue chandeliers being one of the attributes still in the restaurant today.

After a major expansion and reimagining of both the interior and exterior, Broadmoor West reopened in 2014 with Ristorante and Bar del Lago, an entirely new eatery designed by Adam D. Tihany. A mixture of fire and water, Ristorante del Lago has both dining room and patio seating at Bar del Lago—the overlook to the lake accentuated by an outdoor fireplace for even more crackle to the fiery offerings. A pizza and appetizer menu is also offered daily at Bar del Lago, straight from the wood-fired, glass mosaic-encrusted oven. While sipping on a Negroni and sampling the *bianca quattro formaggi*, one almost feels as if they are at Lake Como.

An exhibition kitchen also offers a glimpse into the gastronomic ballet happening behind the scenes, as chefs enter a unique *salumi* and *formaggio* aging room and pull products shipped direct from

Left: *Antipasti misti* (mixed appetizers) include meats straight from Italy.

Top right: Executive Chef David Patterson at the wood-burning oven.

Bottom right: Pasta Bolognese from Ristorante del Lago.

Italy. Cut on a Parma Crown Anniversary Slicer, cured meats meet paired cheeses, while a Sambonet dessert trolley waltzes its way through the dining room.

1 Lake Ave.
719-577-5733
www.broadmoor.com/dining/ristorante-del-lago
Neighborhood: Colorado Springs

IMPERIAL

Open Sesame . . . chicken

The Imperial Chinese Restaurant is the gold standard by which Chinese food is measured in Denver. Since opening its doors in 1985, the Imperial has offered guests white tablecloth service and deliciously spicy Szechwan dishes that keep its following loyal and coming back for more.

Owner Johnny Hsu loved cooking and knew he wanted to be a chef from a young age. Helping his mom cook dinner was a great achievement and one he took very seriously. Hsu served as an apprentice to some of the best chefs in Hong Kong for four years before emigrating to the United States in 1979.

Imperial guardian lions flank the entrance, promising a grand authenticity. The dining room is perfectly dark and red-lacquered. Two large fish tanks with arowana fish for good luck, health, and prosperity—considered auspicious because they resemble Chinese dragons—provide a glow in the background, and everything is quietly efficient.

Must-eats include the tea-smoked Peking duck, all white meat sesame chicken, Hunan beef, hot and sour soup, and the lemon chicken with a sauce that includes the juice of sixty hand-squeezed lemons in each recipe.

> "Cooking and serving the best Chinese food to the American public has always been my dream. I believe dining is the ultimate experience."   –Johnny Hsu

Left: All-white-meat sesame chicken coated in a delicious house-made sauce.

Right: The laughing Buddha welcomes guests. Behind him are engraved chopsticks reserved for frequent guests.

431 S. Broadway
303-698-2800
www.imperialchinesedenver.com
Neighborhood: Baker

THE FORT

Fun on the Front Range

The Fort is an unmistakable Colorado landmark. It was constructed by Samuel P. Arnold in 1962 as a replica of Bent's 1833 Arkansas River fur trade fort. And the family tradition continues within its hallowed walls as Holly Arnold Kinney brings "New Foods of the Old West" to diners, serving up nineteenth-century recipes with contemporary twists.

Dedicated to exploring the trends of the Old West, Yale graduate Samuel P. Arnold began the replica project as a home for his family. Creating the structure authentically down to the hand-formed adobe bricks and handmade furniture by carpenter Elidio Gonzales, Arnold quickly saw his funds dwindle as his aim of living in a living history museum started to slip.

Acquiring a business loan with the condition that a restaurant be added to the building, Arnold designated his wife, who had no restaurant experience, as the chef. The restaurant opened in 1963, and today history comes to life with portions of wild game, rustic recipes, and adaptations from Arnold's impressive historic cookbook collection.

History interpreters, including an American Indian flutist and mountain men in authentic 1880s attire, stroll through the dining room and long-skirted hostesses usher guests to their tables.

Under the direction of William Lumpkins, a renowned architect in adobe construction from Santa Fe, twenty-two men created more than 88,000 adobe bricks by hand from the red clay available on the Fort's property.

Left: The Fort's game plate includes an elk medallion, a buffalo sirloin medallion, and a grilled teriyaki quail.

Top right: Guests enjoy the dining experience in an outdoor teepee.

Bottom right: The Fort's signature dessert, the Negrita, is a blend of dark chocolate whipped with Myers's rum, served in a pewter cup and topped with a cookie.

The Denver Summit of the Eight took place at the Fort in 1997, and plaques commemorating several celebrity diners to the space can be found on the backs of chairs. Another presidential touch is the 1800s White House recipe for Thomas Jefferson's favorite mac 'n' cheese "pudding."

19192 Colorado Hwy. 8
303-697-4771
www.thefort.com
Neighborhood: Morrison

DUFFEYROLL CAFÉ BAKERY

Cinnamon-baked goodness

Duffeyroll was the first food vendor in 16th Street Mall, and Duffeyrolls have been a popular fare in Denver since the 1980s. It grew from one cart to two, one on either end of the mall, and the first brick-and-mortar store opened in 1986 in the Happy Canyon neighborhood. Nick Ault and Jim Duffey named the company after Jim's original cinnamon roll recipe. Buying out Duffey in 1987, Ault kept the name and expanded the flavor offerings. Since then, he's added more flavors, including Mountain Maple, Zesty Orange, and Irish Cream, as well as savory selections, such as Bacon Cheddar and Spinach Tomato.

Expanding into a catering kitchen and additional locations, Duffeyroll continues to be a Denver favorite. Frozen bake-at-home options line a self-serve freezer, and the business sells and ships nationwide. The Duffeyrollers rewards program furthers a sense of community, with beaming photos from years of neighborhood service lining the walls. Ault's grandmother's recipe for Maine island Islesboro iced tea can be purchased by the cup or the gallon.

1290 S. Pearl St.
303-953-6890
www.duffeyrolls.com
Neighborhood: Washington Park

"Our neighborhood meeting place for breakfast and lunch."
—awning at Duffeyroll

Top left: Duffeyroll Café Bakery sits at the north end of historic Pearl Street.

Top right: Nick Ault, president and co-founder.

Bottom: Bakin Sun sandwich with an assortment of Duffeyrolls: Irish Cream, Mountain Maple, the Original, and Zesty Orange.

OLATHE SWEET CORN

Lend me your ear

Each year, everyone looks forward to Olathe sweet corn, the signature white-and-yellow sweet corn trademarked by the Tuxedo Corn Company. Far from the all-yellow varieties of regular corn, the bicolored and even more rare all-white corn pepper menus across the state every summer.

A crossbreed of ancient corn assortments or maize, today's corn is grown on the Western Slope in abundance, with more than thirty million ears harvested every year. Since 1992, corn revelers at the Olathe Sweet Corn Festival have enjoyed live music and corn donated by the Tuxedo Corn Company.

TRY IT

South Pearl Street Farmers Market–Several stalls carry the annual harvest.
Between Iowa and Arkansas on South Pearl Street
303-743-0718
www.southpearlstreet.com/farmers-market

Kroger-branded grocery stores carry most of the Olathe sweet corn in Denver.
www.kroger.com/stores/search

Potager–seasonally driven restaurant that incorporates local ingredients
1109 N. Ogden St.
303-832-5788
www.potagerrestaurant.com

Multi-colored kernels of Olathe sweet corn.

BUCKHORN EXCHANGE

Keep your head at the Buckhorn Exchange

The early days of Denver were a conglomeration of dusty roads, rough neighborhoods, and sometimes even rougher patrons. Located across the street from the Osage Street Rio Grande Railyard and Buckhorn Lodge, the Buckhorn Exchange saw a plethora of colorful characters enter its doors, from cattlemen and miners to Indian chiefs and silver barons. A local watering hole and popular dining spot, the Buckhorn Exchange was visited quite often by Western innovators.

The legendary Buffalo Bill Cody and his traveling troupe of scouts welcomed twelve-year-old Henry Zietz to their ranks in 1877. Nicknamed "Shorty Scout," the future owner of the Buckhorn Exchange became fast friends with Buffalo Bill and his entourage of Indians and scouts, including Chief Sitting Bull. Remnants of his experiences and early days can still be found in the restaurant today, decorating the walls alongside taxidermied trophies from around the globe.

After the Buckhorn Exchange opened in 1893, the now twenty-eight-year old Zietz was quick to recognize the business opportunity for a captive audience of railroaders cashing in their paychecks. Offering tokens for a free lunch and beer each Friday as the men received their wages, Zietz enticed them to the Buckhorn Exchange, where they enjoyed more than one beer to celebrate a week of hard work. Ever evolving and gaining in popularity, the restaurant was visited by then candidate Theodore Roosevelt, the

> Trains still run on tracks near the Buckhorn Exchange, and diners are treated to the old sounds of train horns being blown.

Left: Elk grilled with four-peppercorn crust is farm-raised for the Buckhorn.

Right: Filled with taxidermy and Western memorabilia, the dining room is like no other in Denver.

first of five presidential guests. He suspended his campaign through Denver to go hunting with Henry Zietz on the Western Slope. After enjoying dinner and drinks, he asked Shorty Scout to be his guide to the region.

Photos of Hollywood stars, news anchors, and national celebrities and countless news clippings and articles line the walls of Denver's longest-running restaurant, a reign spanning three centuries. Liquor license No. 1 is still on display, as the restaurant weathered Prohibition and was awarded the first license in the Mile High City, changing the name from saloon to restaurant and bar. Designated as a Denver historic landmark in 1972, the Buckhorn Exchange traded hands from the Zietz family to a local group of investors named the Buckhorn Associates in 1978.

1000 Osage St.
303-534-9505
www.buckhornexchange.com
Neighborhood: Lincoln Park

LOW COUNTRY KITCHEN

Southern charm in LoHi

"Southern hospitality" rolls right off the lips, stirring memories of rich flavors, decadent dishes, and comfort both in food and demeanor. Harkening back to childhoods in Louisiana, Kentucky, and Tennessee, owners Brian and Katy Vaughn embrace a fine-dining background with approachable Southern charm at LOW Country Kitchen.

Originally from Kentucky, Brian moved to Steamboat Springs, Colorado, before graduating from high school. He started working in kitchens at the age of fourteen and continued to do so while skiing the famous champagne powder of Steamboat. Eventually moving to Napa to study at the Culinary Institute of America at age twenty-one, he returned to Colorado after various culinary opportunities throughout the United States. He and Katy opened bistro c.v., specializing in Rocky Mountain cuisine. Seeking the flavors of home, they opened LOW in 2014.

Forty-eight-hour fried chicken, fried green tomatoes, and jambalaya all grace the Southern-inspired menu. A rooftop terrace and outdoor patio below entice diners to enjoy dining al fresco.

1575 Boulder St. A
720-512-4168
www.lowrestaurant.com
Neighborhood: LoHi

Chef Brian Vaughn was invited to cook at the legendary James Beard House in 2016.

Top left: The open-faced fried green tomato BLT features forty-eight-hour pork belly, pimento cheese, and frisée.

Top right: Pecan pie at LOW is a Southern classic.

Bottom left: A handcrafted apron rack near the restaurant's front door creates a welcoming, homey atmosphere.

Bottom right: LOW's signature forty-eight-hour fried chicken features organic, all-natural chicken soaked in buttermilk batter for forty-eight hours. It's then fried to perfection and served with hot sauce.

ESTERS NEIGHBORHOOD PUB

Phish and sports

Opened in 2015, Esters quickly became a neighborhood haunt, with its weekly rotating twenty-two taps being a major draw. Previously from New York, owner Paul Sullivan moved to Colorado in 2002 to work with New Belgium beer. He eventually saw the need for a neighborhood gathering place and struck out to create his own.

The culture of Esters is that of bluegrass music, good beer, and mountain living. Phish fans, of which Sullivan is an avid one, will notice that the pizzas are named after Phish songs. Reclaimed wood can be found throughout the restaurant, with a central polished local tree acting as a community table. The year-round heated patio is a perfect place for lunch or brunch, with a build-your-own Bloody Mary bar a focal point for weekend warriors.

Esters is also a sports bar. Sullivan's hometown team is the Buffalo Bills—a popular team to watch on the big-screen TVs—and World Cup watch parties and bluegrass jams also take over the space. While watching the livestream of the Phish immersive experience, guests can enjoy a unique atmosphere with the food-made-from-scratch kitchen.

Ester is a craft beer term for the sweet, fruity flavors of beer that are created when ethanol is broken down during fermentation.

Sullivan used to work at New Belgium Brewing, and their beer can often be found on tap at Esters.

Above: Esters is the perfect location to order a pizza, enjoy a beer, and visit with friends while watching a game or concert.

Left: Sweet bites found at Esters change seasonally.

The community vibe is equally sweet, as Sullivan participates in school benefits and special tap events to fund nonprofits and community causes.

1950 S. Holly St.
303-955-4904
www.estersdenver.com
Neighborhood: Virginia Vale

DOWNTOWN AQUARIUM

Under the sea at 5,280 feet

A staggering 150,000 gallons of water is enough to quench anyone's thirst, and diners at Downtown Aquarium are greeted with that colossal amount of H_2O. Whether sitting in the main dining room, the Water Room, or the Dive Lounge, 220 guests are able to enjoy a taste of the sea in both spectacle and cuisine.

Floor-to-ceiling exhibits at Downtown Aquarium captivate audiences both young and old with more than eight hundred animal species. Initially opened as Colorado's Ocean Journey in 1999 and funded by a $57 million bond loan and loans from the department of Urban Housing and Development, the aquarium along the South Platte is a destination for families to learn more about the oceans and their wildlife.

After the owners filed for bankruptcy in 2002 with more than $60 million in debt, the aquarium was acquired by Landry's Restaurants, a company boasting more than five hundred properties across the nation. When it opened in 2005, Downtown Aquarium became the largest of the four aquariums owned by Landry's.

Serving eclectic American food, the restaurant in the aquarium is appealing not only to families looking for a group activity but also to adults for date nights or thalassophiles who just want to watch the fish swim by. Homer, the 400-pound grouper, often hangs out

> While open as Colorado's Ocean Journey, the aquarium had a rogue octopus that would sneak out of its enclosure at night to hunt in other tanks. The sneaky mollusk was caught on security cameras.

Top left: Dine next to the large tank and watch a variety of fish swim by your table.

Bottom left: Downtown Aquarium serves a variety of seafood dishes.

Right: The Dive Lounge offers one of Denver's most unique experiences. Look for Homer the grouper, who watches the bartenders as they work.

by the window near the Dive Lounge as cocktails are shaken and served to guests. And in the main dining area, floor-to-ceiling exhibits enchant all those who take time to sit and watch the myriad of fish and sea life.

700 Water St.
303-561-4450
www.aquariumrestaurants.com/downtownaquariumdenver/dining.asp
Neighborhood: Jefferson Park

CLIFF HOUSE

Haute hotel

The gold mining boom of the Pikes Peak area in the 1850s led to a rush of development as incoming miners poured into the region. Nestled at the base of Pikes Peak, Manitou Springs continues to be a destination today. Home to eight mineral springs, the area was frequented by Native Americans who came to drink the naturally carbonated water. Representative of the breath of the great spirit Manitou, the location has long since been a destination for those seeking to cure ills, take in the mountain air, find their fortune, or just relax.

"The Inn," now the Cliff House, opened to guests before Colorado was a state, receiving its first visitors in 1873. A humble twenty-room boarding house, the building grew into a resort for the wealthy in the early 1900s after resident Edward Nichols founded the Manitou Bath House Company. This encouraged a surge of much-needed tourism to the region after the gold strikes and rush started to subside in the area. Notable guests to the now two-hundred-room abode included such names as P. T. Barnum, Clark Gable, J. Paul Getty, and President Theodore Roosevelt. Several of the suites at the hotel have been named for esteemed guests.

Following formal dinners on the property, concerts were held on the front lawn of the hotel. A parade of well-known celebrities and American families flowed in and out of the hotel, and it became a popular destination for the health benefits accredited to the natural springs and for the luxury accommodations. In 1921, a flood ripped

Free collapsible cups are available at the nearby visitors center as well as maps to visit the springs throughout the town to sample the waters.

Left: The historic Manitou Springs destination.

Right: Georges Bank sea scallops, herb risotto, scampi butter, roasted baby fennel, butternut squash, and sun-dried tomatoes.

through the property, and the Cliff House caught fire in 1982. The damage was quickly repaired, but the building stood vacant for the next sixteen years due to a sluggish local economy.

The building was added to the National Register of Historic Places, but despite this recognition, the future of the celebrated space looked bleak. But in the late 1990s, a $10 million renovation was undertaken. The dedication to Rocky Mountain Victorian architecture was carefully tended to, and twenty-first-century amenities were incorporated. The addition of Red Mountain Bar and Grill in 2007 added to the formal dining room experience. Chef Chris Lynch, recipient of the prestigious Four-Diamond Fine Dining Award heads the culinary staff in bringing fresh takes on Colorado ingredients with a fine-dining twist.

306 Canon Ave.
719-785-1000
www.thecliffhouse.com
Neighborhood: Manitou Springs

OLD MAJOR

Deformalized farmhouse dining

Old Major's slogan, "Dedicated to seafood, swine, and wine," accurately sums up the restaurant that features an in-house butchery and charcuterie program, with ingredients sourced from local farms and sustainable seafood offerings.

Chef/owner Justin Brunson is friends with the farmers and fishermen who are the vendor purveyors to his establishment. The restaurant's butchery program utilizes every portion of the animal from nose to tail and cures their meat in-house within a perfectly placed charcuterie room adjacent to the dining room that allows diners to ogle the start of their meal.

Opened in 2013, the three-thousand-square-foot space took over a roller skating rink in LoHi. Dark woods and repurposed aerial photographs of the surrounding area on glass plates make for a unique dining experience while guests tuck in to goat tacos and Colorado bison.

3316 Tejon St.
720-420-0622
www.oldmajordenver.com
Neighborhood: Highlands

Highland townsite was laid out by William Larimer Jr. a month after Denver was founded as a city in 1858.

Top: The well-appointed bar at Old Major.

Bottom left: Executive chef/owner Justin Brunson.

Bottom right: Goat tacos are a crowd pleaser.

CRUISE ROOM

Bottle-shaped bar

One day after Prohibition was repealed in 1933, Denver's legendary Cruise Room opened in the city's oldest hotel—the Oxford Hotel, built in 1891. The Art Deco atmosphere modeled after a lounge on the *Queen Mary* ocean liner is in the shape of a wine bottle and flanked by red neon, chrome accents, and tall murals that stretch to the ceiling.

For ghost hunters, legend has it that a postman sits at the end of the bar, bemoaning delivering holiday gifts in a winter snowstorm. The postman sips a beer while sitting at the bar, but at the end of the night the bartender pick up a still-full can, the postman having disappeared. In the 1930s, the thawed remains of a postman were found in the spring. He had died en route to Central City while attempting to deliver Christmas presents.

A jukebox at the end of the room glows beneath panels depicting the global enjoyment of wine and spirits, with toasts of "cheers" and "good health" translated for patrons. Following World War II, the German panel was ripped from the wall by servicemen fresh back from the war and replaced with an alternate country.

1600 17th St.
303-628-5400
www.theoxfordhotel.com/denver-dining/the-cruise-room
Neighborhood: LoDo

Small plates and hot bites accompany an extensive martini list and historic cocktails shaken by knowledgeable bartenders.

Top left: This unique bar in the heart of Denver boasts a large cocktail menu.

Top right: Chicken drumettes are a perfect snack while enjoying drinks at the Cruise Room.

Bottom left: A jukebox is situated at the end of the narrow, wine-bottle-shaped establishment.

Bottom right: Perfectly crisp fries at the Cruise Room.

DAZZLE

New Orleans–style jazz and spice

Appropriately located in Denver's theater district, Dazzle jazz club fuels fans' need for live music. Jazz-inspired cuisine brings New Orleans flavor to downtown Denver alongside national music acts.

Home to the O. P. Baur Confectionery Company from 1891 to 1970, the building was erected while Colorado was still a territory. Otto P. Baur was a German immigrant whose name became synonymous with old-world quality and attention to detail. He was also charitably minded. His shop is noted for distributing free ice cream cones to children during the Great Depression, and Baur personally served free biscuits to Native Americans camping in Denver in 1860. Added to the Colorado and National Register of Historic Places in 2006, the historic building had sidestepped several eras of demolition and urban renewal plans. In 2017, Dazzle moved from its original location, where it had been since 1998, to the Baur's building.

A collaboration between Miles Snyder and Karen Storck, Dazzle is a jazz institution. Snyder, a jazz lover, and Storck, a chef who wanted to open a restaurant, decided on the Fuji Inn on Lincoln as the original Dazzle location. The Kabuki rooms were converted into stages, and jazz has filled Dazzle's venues ever since, with the partnership of Donald Rossa, the current owner.

Guests to the new location in the Baur's building often come for pre-theater and pre-symphony dinners as well as to watch

At Dazzle, guests can enjoy the stylings of notable jazz artists, such as Eddie Palmieri, Brian Blade, and Cecile McLorin Salvant.

Left: The flat bread is served with Parmesan gelato, sun-dried tomato pesto, and a roasted garlic clove.

Right: Seafood gumbo with crab, rock shrimp, crawfish tails, okra, and basmati rice.

performances in the space itself on one of two stages. The nine-thousand-square-foot space imbues the beauty of a bygone era. Original chandeliers from the 1800s, crown molding, original paintings, and mosaic tile floors form the backdrop for swing dancing and big bands on the Gold Stage as well as smaller sextets on the Chandelier Stage. Chef Mario Godoy, part owner of Dazzle, brings his Italian and Latin background of cooking grace infused with New Orleans–style food for fresh jazz cuisine.

1512 Curtis St.
303-839-5100
www.dazzledenver.com
Neighborhood: Downtown

JILL'S RESTAURANT AND BISTRO

American cuisine with a French accent

Hailing from a town of about eight hundred in the Jura region of France, Chef Laurent Mechin received a postcard when he was eight from a cousin who worked at a resort hotel as a chef. Stirring the imagination of the young chef-to-be, that simple piece of paper launched a career that eventually found him at the helm of Jill's restaurant in Boulder, Colorado.

Young Mechin dived into the inner workings of the kitchen at the age of twelve, when the same cousin who inspired him with that postcard hired him to work in a restaurant he opened in France. The aspiring culinarian was later offered an apprenticeship through the French school system to work in a Michelin three-star restaurant, but he turned it down, as it did not suit his tastes. He decided instead to apprentice at an eight-table restaurant under Chef Pierre Charpentier, and the attention to detail that he learned there continues to influence his cooking and restaurant experience today.

Moving to America after serving in the French Army, Mechin was exposed to an entire onslaught of new food influences and techniques. Far from the foraging, hunting, and gardening ingredients of Jura, he landed in California, where his brother had opened a bakery. He eventually ended up at the Four Seasons hotel group.

Due to the handmade nature of the menu at Jill's, dietary restrictions are easily accommodated, and a variety of vegan,

The Boulder Flatirons geological formation is viewable from the St. Julien property.

Mojo-spiced ruby red trout tacos with red pepper and onion slaw and pineapple cilantro salsa.

vegetarian, and gluten-free dishes are offered. The restaurant's popular tableside service presents a modern and interactive take on a time-honored dining tradition. A number of signature dishes are prepared in dramatic tableside fashion, such as shrimp scampi and grass-fed beef on Himalayan rock salt. Weekly offerings at Jill's Restaurant, such as its Ooh La La Lunch, Vegan Fridays, and Sunday brunch, draw not only hotel guests but also Boulderites and locals from neighboring towns. The beverage program is led by sommelier Antoine Moinard and beverage director Bryan Amaro, and it offers a curated selection of wines, local Colorado beer and spirits, and craft cocktails that incorporate ingredients from the on-site garden.

900 Walnut St.
720-406-7399
www.stjulien.com
Neighborhood: Boulder

COPERTA

When in Rome

D ecorative fountains on the piazzas of Rome conjure up visions of hearty meals, good conversation, and promenades abuzz with visitors going about their day. Across from Benedict Fountain Park, Coperta incorporates some of those Roman values and most of all the fantastic fare found within.

Buffalo mozzarella, Senise peppers, and enticing pastas are all notable, but the pièce de résistance has to be the *pollo alla diavola* or "deviled chicken"—a wood-charred half chicken encircled by vibrant chili oil and spicy marinade. The deceptively large space serves up classic Italian dishes while still feeling quaint. "Coperta," Italian for "blanket," wraps diners in its warm embrace with a focus on subsistence and quality ingredients.

400 E. 20th Ave.
720-749-4666
www.copertadenver.com
Neighborhood: Uptown

The original fountain in Benedict Fountain Park was scrapped in the 1970s, but a replacement made of marble from Carrara, Italy, was installed in 1977.

Top: The spicy *pollo alla diavolo* with chili and piccante oil.

Bottom left: *Spaghetti cacio e pepe* with pecorino romano, cacio di roma, and black pepper.

Bottom right: The Amaro di Amaro cocktail at Coperta.

THE NICKEL

Ticket to ride

It cost you just a nickel to ride a streetcar in 1911. Located in the historic Tramway Building in downtown Denver, the Nickel is now a part of the Hotel Teatro, a boutique hotel in the heart of the city.

Built in 1911 by Fisher & Fisher, the Tramway Building housed the offices of Denver's public transportation system until 1971. The attached streetcar barn, now rehearsal studios for the Denver Center for the Performing Arts, was a bustling hub of activity in the twentieth century. Nearby, in what is now Confluence Park where the Platte River and Cherry Creek converge, was the Denver Tramway Powerhouse, which powered 131 streetcars over 156 miles of track. Closing in the 1950s, the power plant that once burned through more than 170 tons of coal daily became a warehouse for the International Harvester Company and then converted to the Forney Historic Transportation Museum, where streetcars were on display in 1969. After thirty years, the museum moved, and the location is now the Colorado Flagship store for REI. The Platte Valley Trolley still operates Denver trolley cars along the river during the summer, offering a glimpse into the impressive past of the Denver Tramway Company.

Paying homage to Denver's historic American cooking, the Nickel incorporates several unique aspects to the guest's experience here. Barrel-aged cocktails on tap flow behind the bar, which is the centerpiece of the restaurant, as the casks wait patiently above on suspended storage racks. Ingredients from local ranchers, farmers,

Numismatists can visit the nearby Denver Mint, where circulating coins are produced.

Left: The Nickel is located in the Hotel Teatro, stately former home of the Denver Tramway Company.

Right: Seasonally inspired fare found on the menu at the Nickel.

and distillers come together for Colorado cuisine amidst the hustle and bustle of a still busy city. If you listen close enough, you might just hear the bell of a Denver trolley car.

1100 14th St.
720-889-2128
www.thenickeldenver.com
Neighborhood: Downtown

CITY, O' CITY

Terrific tofu

Dan Landes, a creative in every sense of the word, lives his life and imbues his many projects with Daoist principles. He started his restaurant career in 1998 when he opened WaterCourse Foods (the Way of Water) on 13th Avenue. WaterCourse Foods outgrew its original space near the gold-domed capitol, and Landes moved it to Uptown and opened City, O' City in the old WaterCourse location.

In 2015, Landes sold WaterCourse Foods to the general manager of City, O' City, Lauren Roberts, and her mother, Jennifer Byers. Three years later, he sold City, O' City to the same team. Landes himself is off to his next adventure in Puerto Escondido, Oaxaca, Mexico, where he and his family run their vegetarian hostel, Osa Mariposa.

City, O' City still reflects Landes's creativity and philosophical leanings—a place to serve all needs to all people. Vegan? Check. Vegetarian? Gotcha. Gluten-free vegan? Not a problem here. From your 8:00 a.m. almond milk latte to your happy hour cocktail, City, O' City is here to serve. Supporting local artists with rotating monthly in-house gallery shows, City, O' City also features street art–style wall murals both inside and outside the building. Patrons can sit on the patio, and neighboring establishments include a vegan bakery, a boho jewelry boutique, and an upscale resale clothing store, all backdropped by impressive urban street art wall murals.

For those missing their Reubens after giving up meat, a must-try is the seitan pastrami on marble rye. City, O' City's buffalo wrap is another favorite as are their savory "chicken" and waffles. The menu

Left: Gluten-free baked goods at City, O' City.

Right: A seat beneath the central chandelier is a perfect place to grab a bite.

bursts with food that anyone can feel really good about eating, and save room for the Food Network–recommended Ho Ho Cupcake. The interior is quirky, artsy, and eclectic. Layers of color and angles invite exploration. Furnishings and fixtures feature reclaimed and repurposed finds, such as the massive modern chandelier that stretches across an oversized communal table or the soda fountain–style counter chairs. Hipster servers and bartenders are friendly and helpful when answering questions about the vegetarian and vegan offerings. There is no judgment, just low-key assistance. When you get there, you will feel like a guest at the coolest party in Denver surrounded by the most interesting people.

206 E. 13th Ave.
303-831-6443
www.cityocitydenver.com
Neighborhood: Capitol Hill

SAM'S NO. 3

The remaining favorite

Sam's 1–5 all graced the downtown Denver culinary landscape in the 1920s. The five diners were located within five square blocks of one another, and the original Sam's No. 1 on 17th and Curtis had nineteen stools and served one thousand people a day. Still family owned and in their third generation, the diner food continues to draw customers to Sam's No. 3's (now located in Denver, Glendale, and Aurora).

Originally located across the street, Sam's No. 3 is now in the place of the former White Spot restaurant, a popular chain in the '60s. Sam's No. 3 Denver was reopened in 1998. Denver history can be found throughout the expanded space, with the restaurant's Hammer Bar sporting the neon sign that used to be located at Jensen's Hardware just south of Denver University.

1500 Curtis St.
303-534-1927
www.samsno3.com
Neighborhood: Downtown

Momma's Big Fat Omelet is made with six eggs, ham, bacon, sausage, gyro meat, onion, bell pepper, tomato, mushroom, cheddar, Swiss, jack, American, and Kickin' Pork Green Chili. Make sure you're extra hungry if ordering!

Left: The vintage neon sign has a new home at Sam's No 3.

Top right: Kitchen Sink Burrito, which was featured on *Diners, Drive-Ins and Dives*.

Bottom right: Burgers are available with add-ons, such as bacon or eggs, and beef patties can be upgraded to buffalo or veggie patties.

ROAMING BUFFALO BAR-B-QUE

Smoke signals

Coy Webb hails from the Panhandle of Texas, where he practiced BBQ for as long as he can remember. With two firings a day, the popular Roaming Buffalo Bar-B-Que joint sells out quickly, leaving latecomers waiting for the next round of succulent meat to come out of the smoker.

Specialties include bison back ribs, lamb shoulder, and house-made sausage. Brisket is always a popular item as well. Everything is made from scratch, including the sauces, condiments, and jams. The restaurant is a true mom-and-pop operation, and the customer service is often on a first-name basis with regulars and friendly smiles all around for new guests. A bison pelt graces one of the walls, and beetle-kill pine benches line the restaurant.

The building was built in the late '40s/early '50s and is also home to sister restaurant City & County Deli, where Webb curates and sells deli meats.

2387 S. Downing St.
303-722-2226
www.roamingbuffalobbq.com
Neighborhood: Platte Park

Vast herds of American bison—more than sixty million throughout the United States before settlers came to the area—used to roam the plains, river valleys, and prairies of Colorado.

Above: Sausage and sides from Roaming Buffalo
Bar-B-Que.

Right: Ribs all but fall off the bone.

PUNCH BOWL SOCIAL STAPLETON

High-flying fare

Airports are often taken for granted as a staple of any major city. The tented Denver International Airport is an architectural innovation that many have witnessed and experienced. In 1929, farther to the west of the now notable airport, Denver Municipal Airport was opened. Named Stapleton after the mayor of Denver in 1944, the airport became the hub for several major airlines after an expansion, putting Denver firmly on the map as a destination and flight connection point.

Continued growth and some politics saw the development of what is today's Denver International Airport. Air traffic control cleared the last plane at Stapleton on February 27, 1995, and the airport shuttered its doors. A master plan for the redevelopment of the Stapleton area was presented by Denver civic leaders, and Stapleton neighborhoods were born.

Overlooking the entire project burgeoning below was the lonely Air Traffic Control Building, which was deemed too interesting and historic to tear down. With the promising housing development determinedly themed on aviation, the control tower was a welcome aspect to the neighborhood, furthering the theme and nod to history. The 32,000-square-foot property was acquired by Punch Bowl Social, expanding the restaurant concept's operation from its original Broadway location in downtown Denver. Incorporating the

> The first jetliners to fly out of Stapleton were Continental's Boeing 707–style aircraft in 1959.

Left: Chicken 'n' waffles: fried hormone- and antibiotic-free chicken breast and thigh served with a malted waffle, chipotle-citrus maple syrup, and fresh strawberries.

Right: The Knockoff Burger: two grass-fed, hormone-free beef patties topped with American cheese, comeback sauce, pickled onion, and shredded lettuce, served on a sesame seed bun with a side of rosemary fries.

"golden age of flight" into the design, the now centralized hot spot seamlessly integrates itself into the neighborhood.

During construction, owner Robert Thompson started to receive memorabilia saved by locals from Stapleton Airport to use as decor in the beloved behemoth. Flight safety cards, terminal signs, and airport arrival displays all started to show up and were used in the interior design, creating an authentic reminiscence with thoughtful elements. Home to six bowling lanes, ping-pong tables, two private karaoke rooms, a photo booth, shuffleboard, and a variety of indoor and outdoor dining opportunities, Punch Bowl Social has repurposed the original, iconic air traffic control tower.

3120 N. Uinta St.
720-500-3788
www.punchbowlsocial.com/location/stapleton
Neighborhood: Stapleton

FROM A TO Z

ESTABLISHMENTS BY NEIGHBORHOOD

UPTOWN

VIRGINIA VALE

WASHINGTON PARK

WEST COLFAX